The Hunter's Handbook

CRAIG BODDINGTON

MALLARD PRESS

A FRIEDMAN GROUP BOOK

Published by MALLARD PRESS
An Imprint of BDD Promotional Book Company, Inc.
666 Fifth Avenue
New York, N.Y. 10103

Mallard Press and its accompanying design and logo are trademarks of
BDD Promotional Book Company, Inc.

ISBN 0-7924-5461-8

THE HUNTER'S HANDBOOK
was prepared and produced by
Michael Friedman Publishing Group, Inc.
15 West 26th Street
New York, New York 10010

Editors: Stephen Williams and Kelly Matthews
Art Director: Jeff Batzli
Designer: Kingsley Parker
Photography Editor: Ede Rothaus

Typeset by Bookworks Plus
Color separations by Scantrans Pte. Ltd.
Printed and bound in Hong Kong by Leefung-Asco Printers Ltd.

This one for Paula...

Contents

C H A P T E R   O N E

The Hunter's World

Few among us can properly articulate why it is that we hunt. Certainly, in these closing years of the twentieth century, we realize that we no longer need to hunt for our food as our ancestors did. And yet the hunt remains part of us. More than part, for while we do not always hunt, we are always hunters. We see our world through the hunter's eyes.

No rose-colored lenses, these. The hunter stays closer to life's ultimate realities than more urbanized people. The hunter understands the vagaries of a sometimes cruel nature—and thus appreciates its more frequent beauty. The hunter takes little for granted, understanding the gift of nature's bounty, be it a tender steak or a carpet of newly fallen leaves. And the hunter learns to observe, closely and constantly, truly *seeing* the world, not just passing through it.

The hunter sees the forests, plains, deserts, and mountains of his world, and the skies as well—the patterning of the constellations on a starry night, the deep blue of higher altitudes, and the changing weather foretold by building clouds. In part, it is true, the hunter sees the world with a predatory eye for, like all predators, human eyes are close set and forward looking. But the hunter accepts this as natural and isn't limited by it. The hunter, being a reasoning human, also sees the world through the eyes of a caretaker.

The hunter knows that only humans have so altered the world that nature's course cannot maintain a balance without the further influence of humans. The hunter accepts the role of steward of the wild things and wild places. In generations past, hunters created the concept of conservation and virtually alone poured their time, effort, and

Thanks to modern game management—conceived by hunters and paid for with hunters' dollars—virtually all of rural North America is part of the hunter's world. In few other corners of this planet can sportsmen so readily enjoy the variety and abundance of game available to North American hunters.

For some, hunting is very much a family affair. Others prefer to hunt alone or perhaps with a good friend. Whether shared or not, the act of hunting is a very personal experience, almost impossible to explain to persons who do not hunt.

© Will Brewster

finances into maintaining—and often saving—the wildlife and habitat we all enjoy.

Today the hunter is beset by strong enemies— well-organized, outspoken anti-hunters, preservationists, animal rightists—and perhaps isn't responding as strongly as hunting's foes. The problem is that the hunter is not outspoken by nature. The hunter finds it almost beyond belief that the validity of hunting should be questioned—and thus finds it almost impossible to objectively defend. Casting emotions aside, the hunter knows the facts and figures, knows of the millions upon millions of dollars that hunters have spent toward conservation, and knows the success of those efforts. The

hunter lives them. But emotions cannot be cast aside with so personal an issue as the question of hunting, so the hunter becomes frustrated when documented truths fall before the anti-hunters' often outrageous lies. And, regrettably, the hunter often keeps his identity as a hunter hidden within himself. Nor is the hunter well organized; hunters are individualists who pursue a most solitary sport.

Largely for these reasons, it is said that the hunter is a vanishing species. In these closing years of this century, indeed a smaller percentage of the human race hunts than ever has before. But hunters find it inconceivable that their tribe might vanish, for they know no other way to see their

world. Hunters may never become outspoken defenders of their cause, and it seems unlikely that they will ever become as well organized as their enemies. But in this ever more urbanized world, with fewer youngsters growing up in the way of the hunter, hunters *must* become teachers if they are to survive; they must learn how to pass along their skills and unique vision. Therein rests the future of hunting, and indeed the future of the game and wild places that hunters protect. For if not we hunters, then who?

No longer can the hunter enjoy the sport at will, as was done in the early days of this country. Today's seasons are often short, and certainly bag limits are restricted. But hunters themselves created these restrictions so that they and future generations could enjoy their sport. And thanks to such foresight, whatever the future may hold, the hunter's world today is very broad indeed.

Never before in this century has so much deer hunting been so readily available to so many American hunters. Thanks to modern game management—funded by hunters' dollars—white-tailed deer are more plentiful than ever before, with seasons becoming longer and bag limits more liberal by the year. In the West, too, elk and mule deer populations are stable or increasing, and concentrated efforts are paying big dividends with more scarce species such as bighorn sheep, mountain goat, and moose.

It's true that drought coupled with overdevelopment of wetlands has led to a significant decline in duck populations, a decline that must be halted. But geese populations are at an all-time high in this century and are increasing, and once-rare waterfowl such as tundra swans and sandhill cranes again offer a surplus. Upland birds, beneficiaries of the edge habitat where agriculture joins cover, have suffered from intensive farming. But thanks to the government's Conservation Reserve Program (CRP), the 1990s promises to be the best decade for quail, pheasant, and grouse in a half century.

The wild turkey, once virtually gone from America's forests and plains, is today's hunter-conservationist's latest and one of his greatest success stories. From coast to coast, the hills and hollows in spring echo with the wild turkey's gobble, and turkey hunting is fast becoming a springtime tradition once again.

While most hunters do indeed enjoy most of their hunting close to home, even as their forebears did, the hunter's world today knows virtually no boundaries. The modern world, with its rapid transportation and instantaneous communication,

Several years of drought in Canadian nesting grounds coupled with the loss of wetland habitat have created a genuine crisis for North American duck populations. This is one of very few dark clouds in the extremely bright picture of North American game today. Duck populations remain huntable, but reduced bag limits, shorter seasons, and more hunter effort are the short-term future of waterfowl hunting.

© Tony Mandile

Thanks to modern transportation, today's hunter is within reach of a whole world of adventure—including this moonlit elk basin in the Rockies, above.

has brought within reach of the average hunter adventures previous generations only dreamed of. The wilds of Alaska and Canada are more accessible than ever before, yet remain the true wilderness every hunter longs to see. Nor does the hunter's world end with the North American continent. From the Alps of Europe to the Southern Alps of New Zealand; from the slopes of Mount Kilimanjaro to the Kalahari Desert; from the mountains of Asia to Australia's outback—never before has so much adventure been so easily reached and available to the hunter.

Hunting equipment, too, has never been better or more available. Sporting arms are at an unprecedented level of performance, and technological advances in fibers have made hunting clothing more effective than ever in protecting its wearer from the elements. Even hunting techniques have changed today, as new knowledge of wildlife habits and habitat becomes available to hunters.

Yes, the hunter's world is changing—but it remains a great world for today's hunter, with more to learn and more to see than ever before. Ours is a sport rich in tradition, but the equipment we use and even our hunting techniques have changed with the times. In the following chapters, we'll examine not only the many diverse aspects of our fascinating sport, but also the arms and equipment available to today's hunter.

© Craig Boddington

Most hunters enjoy dreaming of such far away lands as the windswept Southern Alps of New Zealand, above—and today's hunters have a better chance of making those dreams come true than sportsmen of any previous generation.

CHAPTER   TWO

Modern Hunting Arms

Whether one is a squirrel hunter, bird hunter, or big-game hunter—or, like most of us, some combination of these and more—and whether the chosen arm is a shotgun, rifle, handgun, or bow, that piece of equipment is the hunter's single most essential tool. To some hunters, that's all the gun or bow is: a tool, much the same as a shovel or hammer. To others, perhaps to most, the hunting arm is much, much more. Though still a tool, it's an object of fascination and endless study. The hunting arm of today has many forms and variations; to the hunter fascinated by this tool, the exact choice of arm becomes an extension of the person, a statement of personality.

There's nothing wrong with this fascination with hunting arms. It's part of the fun, and deliberations over the exactly perfect gun and load or broadhead design have sparked campfire discussions for generations. But it must be understood that there is no one perfect tool for a particular hunting situation. There are indeed arms ill suited to specialized conditions, but within very broad limitations, it's difficult to have the wrong gun or bow. Most modern sporting arms are versatile tools, best suited to certain situations but adequate for many.

So long as the arm chosen is reasonably adequate for the job at hand, far more important than its physical characteristics—its exact caliber, gauge, draw weight, or the projectile it uses—is the skill of its user. Regrettably, this is an age where we try to replace practice with power, skill with technology. Today's sporting arms are indeed marvelous pieces

The shotgun is perhaps the most basic of all hunting tools. Unlike a hunting rifle, however, neither its sights nor its accuracy can be improved, nor can you handload custom-tailored ammunition for it. On the other hand, the shotgun is much more frequently the recipient of such embellishments as the fine scrollwork on this classic side-by-side double (opposite).

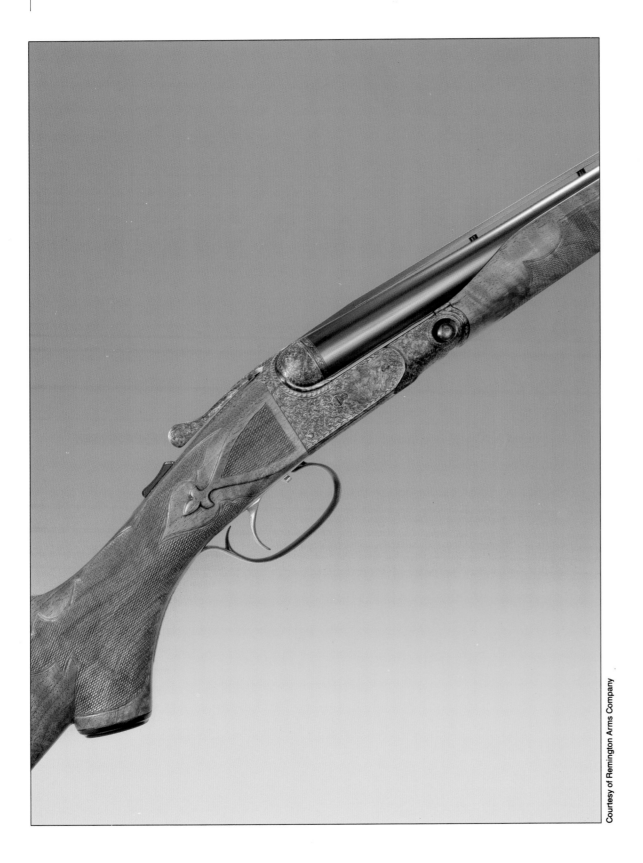

Courtesy of Remington Arms Company

of equipment—more accurate and reliable than ever before (like their ammunition). But there remains no substitute for shooting skill, and there are no shortcuts.

Whatever your chosen arm, the only path to proficiency lies in frequent and continued practice. Proficiency through practice is especially important for the hunter, for in the game fields the shooting is infinitely varied, and the hunter is frequently tired or short of breath and shooting in poor light. Most important, though, is the fact that the hunter has an obligation to take game cleanly and efficiently. And the only way to do that consistently is through shooting skill, whatever your choice of arm might be. Here's a look at the various types of modern hunting arms.

Shotguns

The shotgun is perhaps the most basic hunting tool. Unlike a rifle, neither its sights nor its aiming point can be changed readily. Nor can its ammunition be custom-tailored in the same way it can be for a handloaded rifle or pistol. Nor can shooting a bird on the wing with a shotgun be compared to more deliberate shooting done with either rifle or bow. Wingshooting is indeed an art rather than a science, a game of smooth, consistent motion and perfect timing. The shotgun becomes an extension of the arm and eye, and while the gun's action type and gauge makes little difference, the way it fits the shooter is absolutely critical. While rifle shooting involves the deliberate aligning of sights, shotgunning is much more instinctive.

There are five basic shotgun types in common use today: single shot, bolt action, slide action, semiautomatic, and double barrel. The single-shot hunting shotgun (as opposed to sophisticated and expensive single-barrel competition guns) is perhaps the most basic tool of all. Simple, reliable, safe, and inexpensive, such a gun is often chosen as a learning tool for beginning hunters, but is rarely the choice of an experienced shooter. Much the same could be said of the bolt-action shotgun, but in fairness to both types it should be added that with proper chokes and loads either will take game most effectively. And their relative slowness compared to other action types tends to make their users careful of their shots—never a bad habit!

The slide, or pump action, is almost exclusively American, seen almost nowhere else in the world. And yet this is a fast and dependable repeating shotgun action—quite possibly the fastest of all for repeat shots. To

cycle the action after firing, the supporting hand works the fore-end back and then forward again. Attached to the bolt through action rods, this movement of the fore-end thus actuates the cycle of unlocking, extraction, ejection, loading, and lockup.

Trick shooters have proven for decades that a manually operated pump gun is faster than an automatic, but there's another, much more subtle advantage to the slide action. Wingshooting, especially very fast shooting such as for quail or grouse, depends largely on eye-hand coordination. That forward action of the supporting hand is toward the target, and I believe it unconsciously directs the gun barrel onto the bird even as the action is being closed. But whether you believe that or not, at least believe that nothing is as fast as an experienced shooter with a pump!

Semiautomatic shotguns, in which the action automatically cycles (ejects the spent shell and loads a new one) after firing, generally are one of two types: recoil activated or gas operated. Obviously

The Parker AHE side-by-side 20 gauge on the opposite page is newly manufactured by Remington's Custom Shop, a real departure in today's world with almost no side-by-sides being made in America. Weatherby's excellent Athena over/under, shown above in a Grade V version, is, like most double shotguns today, manufactured overseas.

What's a Gauge?

While calibers are expressed either in millimeters or hundredths or thousandths of an inch, shotgun gauges are calculated by a very old English system based on the number of round balls of that bore diameter that are required to make up a pound. The 16-gauge, for instance, means that sixteen round balls fitting that bore diameter add up to one pound. Or, to put it another way, a round ball fitting a 16-gauge weighs one ounce. In the case of the 12-gauge, twelve balls equal one pound, so each round 12-gauge ball weighs one and one-third ounces. This traditional system holds for all our modern shotgun gauges except the .410, which is actually a caliber rather than a gauge.

The larger the gauge (meaning the *smaller* the gauge number), the more shot the load can contain—meaning that game-killing pattern densities reach out a bit farther. However, each *pellet* has essentially the same velocity and the same energy, whether fired from a .410 or a 10-gauge; neither shoots *farther* than the other, but the 10-gauge's much greater amount of shot will throw an effective pattern much farther.

some force must do the mechanical work of moving the heavy bolt back and forth. With recoil-activated shotguns, such as the classic Browning Auto-5, it's simply the harnessed force of recoil, acting through a long recoil spring, that moves the bolt backward and then forward. The vast majority of today's auto-loading shotguns are gas operated, using small quantities of burning powder gases, bled off through ports in the barrel, to operate the action.

Recoil-operated auto-loaders tend to be a bit more reliable and less sensitive to fouling, while the action of a gas-operated gun tends to lessen recoil somewhat. The auto-loader is popular and efficient, and is available in a tremendous range of makes and models today.

Double barrels come in two basic configurations: side-by-side and over/under. In either case, the action may be the simpler box-lock or the side-lock, which is generally handmade. The latter is easily distinguished by its extended side plates, usually used as a medium for engraving and other embellishment. Likewise, either a side-by-side or an over/under may have double or single triggers, and a single-trigger gun may or may not offer the ability to select one barrel or the other to fire first. A double gun may be built with selective ejectors, ejecting the fired barrel only, or it may have just extractors.

The double barrel's strong suit, whether side-by-side or over/under, is offering two barrels and two actions joined together on one stock. A double gun

with two triggers offers instantaneous choice of different chokes—or, for that matter, shot sizes. And of course, no action type is as fast for the second shot.

Side-by-side fans love its broad sighting plane, slim profile, and quick handling abilities. While inexpensive side-by-sides are available, the side-by-side has been the classic form of the world's finest and most expensive shotguns. In America there were fine doubles such as Parker, L.C. Smith, and the Winchester Model 21, while the fine English firms such as Holland and Holland and Purdey will still make a double gun to the maker's specifications—for a bit more than the price of a luxury car!

Although the side-by-side is held in reverence by many, shotgunners who grew up with pumps and autos sometimes have trouble getting the hang of the two-barrel sighting plane. That's no problem with the over/under; it offers a single sighting plane with all the other advantages of a side-by-side. The only slight disadvantage the over/under has in comparison with a side-by-side is that due to its configuration, it cannot be built quite as light. While there are both very plain and very expensive over/unders, the typical stack barrel is a bit more costly than a repeater but not beyond the reach of most.

While the variations are endless, shotgun hunting takes four basic forms. These are so different that the hunter choosing a shotgun must take into consideration the gun's primary use.

Upland Bird Guns

Upland bird hunting generally means grouse, woodcock, quail, dove, and pheasant—fast-flying birds, usually hunted on the rise. Ranges are more often short than long, and the shooting is fast. While any of the repeaters are satisfactory, upland bird hunting is the twin-barreled gun's strongest suit. Rarely is there time or need for more than two shots, but those two shots should be available as quickly as possible—and there are occasions when the instantaneous choice of chokes with a double-triggered gun could be valuable.

The 12-gauge is the universal gauge. But the upland gun must be carried more than it will be shot, and especially given the effectiveness of today's ammunition, most hunters would be equally well served by a lighter 16- or 20-gauge gun. Expert shots can do amazingly well with the little 28-gauge, but even in expert hands, the .410 should be limited to quail over dogs and dove hunting.

Since most upland bird shooting will be done in a fast-breaking situation, stock fit, or the way the gun rests against the shoulder, is extremely important. Most hunters do best with a slightly high stock comb. Stocked in this fashion, the eye will look slightly down on the rib and bead, and the gun will shoot slightly high. On rising birds, this will prevent you from shooting underneath them—and you won't have to cover them up with the gun barrel to hit them. Instead you'll place the bird just on top of your front bead, a much more natural aim.

Shotgun Chokes

Many years ago it was discovered that the rate of dispersion of a shotgun's pellets could be controlled by a slight degree of constriction at the muzzle. No constriction at all is called a cylinder choke; a gun bored this way should keep just 30 percent of its pellets within a thirty-inch circle at forty yards. The maximum amount of constriction possible is called full choke; such a gun should keep 80 percent of its pellets within the same circle. Between cylinder and full are improved cylinder, modified, and improved modified chokes.

Traditionally, the improved cylinder choke has been the choice for close-range shotgunning, such as hunting grouse and quail. Full choke has been the waterfowler's choice, while modified has been considered an all-around choke.

Today the water is muddied tremendously by the requirement in many areas to use steel shot. (Due to environmental concerns regarding the use of lead, steel shot seems likely to be an increasing part of shotgunning in the future.) The much harder steel doesn't compress in a shotgun barrel the same way as lead. It tends to pattern much more tightly—but is easy to "overchoke," especially with coarse shot.

Today, if steel shot is to be used, most factories recommend you drop down one degree of choke from what you're accustomed to with lead. In other words, if you usually shoot full choke, go to improved modified or modified with steel.

Today's interchangeable choke tubes are wonderful devices, giving shotgunners flexibility never known before. However, just as a rifleman sights in the rifle, the savvy shotgunner will head to the pattern board and actually determine how the shotgun patterns before heading afield with it.

© Will Brewster

Steel Versus Lead

As with chokes, the switch to steel requires some adjustment in selection of shot sizes. The lighter steel loses its velocity more quickly than lead and will not penetrate as well in the same shot size. In general, if you use steel shot two shot sizes larger than lead, you should have results similar to what you're used to. The following is a general guide.

GAME	RECOMMENDED SHOT SIZES	
	LEAD	STEEL
Quail, Dove	7½, 8	6
Pheasant, Decoyed Ducks	6	4
Pass-Shooting Ducks	4	2
Decoyed Geese	2	BB
Pass-Shooting Geese	BB	T

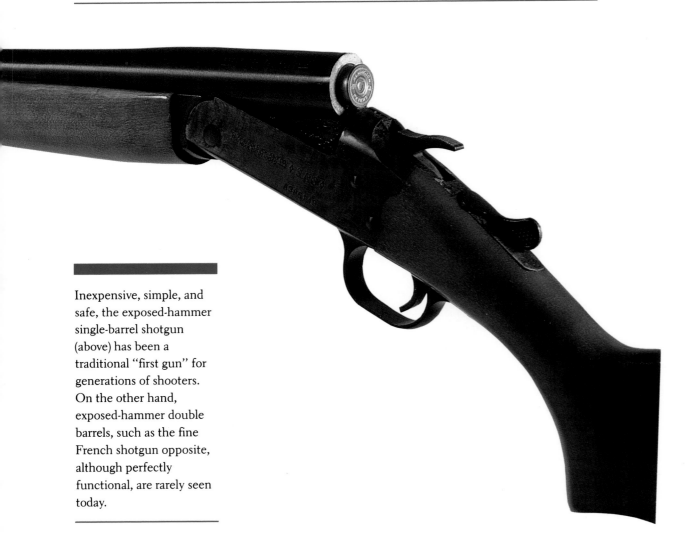

Inexpensive, simple, and safe, the exposed-hammer single-barrel shotgun (above) has been a traditional "first gun" for generations of shooters. On the other hand, exposed-hammer double barrels, such as the fine French shotgun opposite, although perfectly functional, are rarely seen today.

Waterfowl Guns

Hunting waterfowl is a much more deliberate game. And generally it's done from a fixed position, a blind, so gun weight isn't important. Shooting can be much farther, and waterfowl often come in large flocks, so repeat shots might be desirable.

Again, any action type will do, but the nod goes to pumps and autos. Which one depends on personal preference; I prefer the reliability of the pump, while others like the recoil reduction of a gas-operated auto-loader. The gun weight also soaks up a bit of recoil, and the extra-long sighting plane of the barrel plus the action is desirable for this deliberate type of shooting.

Especially with today's requirement to shoot steel shot, waterfowl hunting is for the largest gauges—12-gauge and the big 10-gauge.

Wild Turkey Hunting

Due to the very size of the bird, wild turkey hunting is only for 10- and 12-gauge guns, choked as tightly as possible. There is no need for repeat firepower, but there is certainly the need for a second, follow-up shot as quickly as possible. My own idea of the perfect turkey gun is a double-barreled, double-triggered 10-gauge or 12-gauge magnum, thus offering the option of fine shot in one barrel for a head shot and coarse shot in the second barrel for a body shot or fast follow-up.

Shotguns for Deer

Millions of hunters are obligated by law to use shotguns for deer hunting. Excepting a few very specialized situations, slugs are the way to go; buckshot is extremely ineffective, except at very close range. And of course slug shooting is a 12-gauge game; it's in that gauge that all the recent developments have become available. In the past, there was little option for hunters but to have Foster-type hollow-base slugs rattle down their barrels and hope for the best, but in the past few years, there have been tremendous advances in slug-shooting technology. First off, the slug shotgun should have good adjustable rifle sights—and a low-powered scope is even better. Most of the major manufacturers offer pump and semiautomatic shotguns so configured from the factory—or aftermarket barrels with good sights. Because of the problem in getting the two barrels to shoot closely together with a single projectile, double barrels should not be considered for slug use.

Whatever gun is chosen, the hunter should experiment with every brand and type of slug he can get his hands on to find out what groups best in that shotgun. Those willing to invest a bit more money should consider one of the aftermarket rifled slug barrels, or "paradox" barrels or choke tubes with just the last few inches rifled. Such devices, coupled with new ammo, have done wonders for slug accuracy. Today's slug gun should be

© Guy Marche/FPG International

accurate to 100 yards, and often beyond, but hunters who must rely on slugs should treat their guns just like a long-range hunting rifle, experimenting endlessly with loads to wring the utmost in performance from their deer shotgun.

Cartridges for centerfire rifles can indeed be confusing, with a myriad of different cases for the same bullet diameter—and no hard-and-fast rules exist for naming cartridges. These are just a few of the more common .30-caliber cartridges, from top: .300 Weatherby Magnum, .300 Winchester Magnum, .30-06 Springfield, .308 Winchester, and .30-30 Winchester.

Hunting Rifles and Cartridges

Rifles for game run the gamut from very small to very large; from .22s for small game up to very large, very powerful rifles for the world's largest and most dangerous game. At their smallest and largest, hunting rifles are much like shotguns— basic tools, with few options available for improving performance with sighting equipment or handloaded ammunition. In between lies the whole spectrum of centerfire hunting rifles—rifles for long-range hunting of varmint, deer, bear, elk, sheep, pronghorn, moose, caribou, and all the other types of game in the world. The rifles in this category are perhaps the most fascinating hunting tools, for they can be rebedded or restocked, their sights or scopes changed, and their ammunition infinitely varied and tailored for the exact situation at hand. Most hunting rifles are exceptionally versatile tools; there is no such thing as a deer rifle that isn't suited for any other type of hunting, but some rifle types, as well as calibers, are better suited for certain types of hunting. The same five action types found with shotguns are found with rifles—single shot, slide action, semiautomatic, bolt action, and, rarely, double barrel. To these is added the all-American lever action. Unlike shotguns, however, which have just six common gauges, there are dozens upon dozens of centerfire rifle cartridges and a bewildering array of calibers and case designs, many of which are very similar or even overlap in purpose. Before looking at the rifles themselves, it's absolutely essential to briefly examine this confusing world of centerfire hunting cartridges.

Varmint Cartridges

Varmint hunting is generally the dispatching of nonedible pests ranging from ground squirrels and prairie dogs up through woodchucks all the way to coyotes. This game requires precision shooting, and there's a whole class of cartridges designed to handle such work. Primarily these are the .22 centerfires, with the .17 Remington below and light-bullet loads in the 6 millimeter and .25s above. In some states, these cartridges will be legal for deer-size game, but in most, they're not. Whether legal or not, their light, fast, fragile bullets are ill-suited for use on large game. Yes, careful hunters who pick their shots can work wonders with them, but they should be put to their intended use: precision shooting at smaller game at long range.

Close-Cover Cartridges

This group of cartridges is relatively low in velocity, designed for short-range use on deer-size game and larger, in thick cover. Such cartridges include such classic "oldies" as the .30–30 Winchester, .35 Remington, and .45–70.

Open-Country Cartridges

This is the full gamut of general-purpose flat-shooting hunting cartridges—general purpose because a cartridge well suited for open country will perform yeoman service at close range as well. In caliber, this group starts with the heavy-bullet, 6-millimeter loads, and it works its way on up to the flatter-shooting .33s and .35s. In general, the smaller calibers in this group, say .243 through .270, are limited to use on deer-size game, while the larger cartridges will handle game up through elk and moose.

Dangerous-Game Cartridges

This is a most specialized category. It begins with the .338 Winchester Magnum as a sensible minimum for big bears, goes on up to the .375 Holland and Holland Magnum as a minimal all-around dangerous-game rifle, then continues to the big boomers, suited for anything that walks: the .416s, .458 Winchester Magnum, and the mostly obsolete British Nitro-Express cartridges.

The following table shows a selection of cartridges within each class.

Cartridges

There are simply no hard-and-fast rules governing how cartridges are named, and with today's almost innumerable sporting cartridges, it's no wonder there's a lot of confusion. A rifle barrel has two diameters: the diameter between the lands, or the raised portion of the rifling, and the slightly larger groove diameter. This groove diameter is also the bullet diameter. Both of these dimensions have traditionally and somewhat indiscriminately been used to name cartridges. In the blackpowder era, the charge of blackpowder was added, and finally the original manufacturer's or designer's name is given.

The .30–30 Winchester, for instance, is a .30-caliber, originally charged with thirty grains of black powder, and it was designed by Winchester. However, the .30–30 uses .308-caliber bullets, as does the .30–06 (06 standing for government cartridge of 1906). So does the .308 Winchester, which uses bullet diameter for its name.

The .250 Savage is a .25-caliber using a .257-inch bullet—and so is the .257 Roberts, but each has a different case. And sometimes cartridge names and actual bore *or* bullet diameter mean little. The .44 Magnum and .444 Marlin fire the same bullets, but from different cases. However, their bullets are actually .430-inch in diameter. It is confusing—which is why it's essential to make sure you know what you're buying when you purchase cartridges, and only use ammunition marked with the same *exact* cartridge designation as shown on the rifle's barrel.

As reflected in this chart, there is a wide variety of sporting cartridges suited for nearly any type of hunting. Some shoot a bit flatter and some hit a bit harder—and these things are paid for in greater noise and recoil. Within reasonable limits, hunters should always be more concerned with shooting skill and shot placement than with the exact paper ballistics of their cartridge.

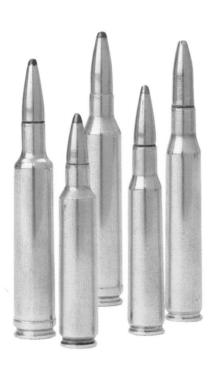

POPULAR SPORTING CARTRIDGES BY CLASS

CARTRIDGE	BULLET WEIGHT (in grains)	VELOCITY MUZZLE	(FPS) 200 YDS	ENERGY MUZZLE	(FT LBS) 200 YDS
VARMINT CARTRIDGES					
.17 Rem.	25	4040	2646	906	389
.22 Hornet	45	2690	1505	723	226
.223 Rem.	55	3240	2304	1282	648
.22-250	55	3680	2654	1654	860
.243 Win.	80	3350	2593	1994	1194
CLOSE-COVER CARTRIDGES					
.30-30	150	2390	1685	1903	946
.35 Rem.	200	2080	1377	1922	842
.358 Win.	200	2490	1875	2754	1562
.444 Marlin	265	2120	1405	2645	1162
.45-70	300	1880	1416	2355	1335
OPEN-COUNTRY CARTRIDGES					
.243 Win.	100	2960	2449	1946	1333
.25-06 Rem.	117	2990	2487	2323	1607
.270 Win.	130	3060	2560	2704	1892
.270 Wby. Mag.	130	3375	2878	3289	2391
.280 Rem.	150	2890	2373	2783	1877
7mm-08 Rem.	140	2860	2402	2543	1794
7mm Rem. Mag.	160	2950	2517	3093	2252
.307 Win.	150	2760	1923	2538	1231
.308 Win.	150	2820	2262	2649	1705
.30-06	165	2800	2283	2873	1911
.300 Wby. Mag.	180	3300	2865	4354	3282
DANGEROUS-GAME CARTRIDGES					
.338 Win. Mag.	250	2660	2261	3929	2839
.340 Wby. Mag.	250	3000	2621	4997	3814
.375 H&H	270	2690	2162	4339	2803
.416 Rem. Mag.	400	2400	1962	5117	3420
.458 Win. Mag.	500	2040	1526	4622	2587

Figures reflect published factory ballistics; wherever possible, spitzer bullets were used.

Hunting Bullets

Regardless of choice of cartridge, it's the bullet that actually does the work—and a cartridge's performance has much to do with your choice of bullet.

Flat-pointed and round-nosed bullets tend to open quickly and transfer energy more dramatically than sharp-pointed (spitzer) designs. They're great in brush, but their poor aerodynamics make a significant difference in ballistics at ranges past 150 to 200 yards. For all-around use, then, a spitzer design is the best. But which one?

Every major manufacturer offers its own line of soft-point bullets: Winchester's Power Point, Remington's Core-Lokt, Federal's Hi Shok, and so on. All are pretty good, but there are also several "premium" lines of ammunition on the market today; not only Federal's Premium, but also Winchester's Supreme, and Remington's new Extended Range ammo. These lines cost more and may or may not be worth it in your rifle.

Every rifle is a rule unto itself, and there's no predicting what brand of ammo, bullet weight, or style will perform best in any given rifle. Hunters who wish to shoot factory ammunition should experiment with as many different loads as possible to see what groups best in their rifle. However, accuracy is one issue, and performance on game is quite another. Most popular calibers offer extremely light bullets designed for varmints as well as a range of game bullets. Stay away from the light bullets, selecting instead medium to heavy bullets for your caliber. And if you're after game larger than deer, consider paying that little bit extra for one of the premium-grade loads.

Handloading for Hunting

Factory ammunition today is extremely good; so good that it's hard to improve on. And in most popular calibers there's a broad enough choice of good bullets to satisfy almost anyone. And yet a great many serious hunters handload their hunting ammo. Why?

Handloading offers the opportunity to custom-tailor ammunition to a particular rifle or hunting situation. In some cases, factory velocity can be improved upon; in other cases, better accuracy can be obtained. And of course there's a much wider choice of bullets available to the handloader. Including super-premium bullets offering unusually outstanding performance. The fascination and the challenge is to create the perfect load. And in the creation of such a load, one develops an unusual level of confidence in the rifle and that load.

One can save a bit of money through handloading and thus shoot more. And it's possible that there is a measurable increase in performance and accuracy. What handloading really brings the hunter is added confidence—the knowledge that the rifle and its load are perfect for the job at hand.

Savage 99

Ruger Number One

Remington Model 700

Lever-Action Rifles

The classics of this American favorite are the saddle guns made by Winchester and Marlin. Typically chambered for our "close-cover cartridges," these light, fast-handling rifles make simply marvelous deer rifles in country where shots won't exceed 100 to 125 yards. Rifles of this type are also available in larger cartridges, well suited for black bear, elk, and even moose—but only at very close range. These rifles are chambered for a couple of very good general-purpose cartridges as well, especially the newer .307 Winchester. However, their tubular magazine requires the use of flat-pointed bullets. The poor aerodynamic design of this bullet shape makes the performance capability of these cartridges moot.

Then there are the other lever-actions, those designed for high-intensity cartridges firing sharp-pointed aerodynamic bullets. There have been several, but the two that remain are the Savage Model 99, an old-timer, and Browning's slick little BLR. Both are chambered to cartridges well suited for general big-game hunting, and both use box magazines and thus can safely handle sharp-pointed bullets.

Typically, the two-piece stock of a lever-action limits accuracy somewhat, although today's lever guns are plenty accurate for most hunting needs. Other drawbacks include limited camming power for extracting sticky cases, meaning that handloaders have to stay with mild loads, and triggers that for safety reasons have to be left fairly stiff and often creepy. In spite of these problems, the lever gun remains popular and is a viable choice in all but the most open terrain.

Slide-Actions and Semiautos

These can be considered together, for indeed there is just one slide-action centerfire remaining today: Remington's Model 760/7600 series. It's a sound rifle chambered to high-intensity cartridges suitable for any big game short of the big bears, and like the pump shotgun, the slide-action rifle is exceedingly fast. It has the same limitations of the lever gun but still retains quite a following—especially in the eastern whitetail woods.

The semiautomatic hunting rifle is only slightly more popular, with just a handful of models available. Browning's BAR gas-operated semiauto is chambered to powerful magnum cartridges suited for anything in North America, and indeed both it and its Remington counterpart have achieved some popularity. Today's semiauto designs are exceedingly reliable and surprisingly accurate. And obviously they're very fast for second and subsequent shots.

Bird hunters who use pump or semiauto shotguns and wish to do some casual deer or other big-game hunting might be well advised to stick with a

From top, the Savage 99 lever action, Ruger Number One single shot, and Remington's Model 700 bolt action all have totally different action types, but each is a perfectly suitable general-purpose hunting rifle. All offer adequate accuracy and all are chambered for cartridges suited for close, medium, and even long-range hunting.

Custom-made .458

familiar action. Serious handloaders tend to stay away from both action types due to accuracy limitations and relatively weak extraction, and there's another problem that needs to be mentioned. The semiautomatic action can't be "babied"; for it to work properly, the bolt must be slammed home when loading, not eased forward as you do with a manual action. This is very noisy, thus a semiauto must be carried loaded with full reliance on the mechanical safety. That's fine for stand hunting but a poor practice for hunting on foot in rough terrain.

Single-Shots

The single-shot was virtually gone until Bill Ruger brought out his wonderful Number One single-shot twenty-odd years ago. It was an instant success, and today Browning and Thompson/Center also offer modern single-shots. Available in cartridges spanning the full range of hunting needs from prairie dogs to elephants, the modern single-shot is simple, accurate, dependable, and offers extremely attractive lines. Its limitation, that of offering just a single shot, is also its strength; the attraction of the one-shot concept of careful marksmanship is strong. And without question, the knowledge that just the one shot is readily available makes one a more careful hunter!

Double Rifles

This action type is exceedingly rare in America. Double-barreled rifles, whether side-by-side or over/under, are extremely costly to build. The difficulty lies in getting the barrels to shoot to the same point of aim, and almost no double will offer the accuracy of any other action type. Still, they do offer adequate field accuracy for short-range work, and no other action offers as fast or as foolproof a second shot. Europeans often use doubles in medium calibers for general big-game hunting, and certainly such a rifle would be at home in the whitetail woods. But Americans tend to regard the double rifle strictly as a heavy-caliber affair for dangerous game, a charge-stopping rifle. It will certainly do this, but a big bolt action will do the same at one-tenth the cost. The least expensive doubles cost about the same as an average car; the most expensive the same as an average house. Thus they remain uncommon but offer a magical charisma all their own.

Bolt-Actions

The bolt-action rifle embodies the ultimate development of the sporting rifle, and this is far and away the most popular type of rifle action available today. Its basic advantages are strength of action,

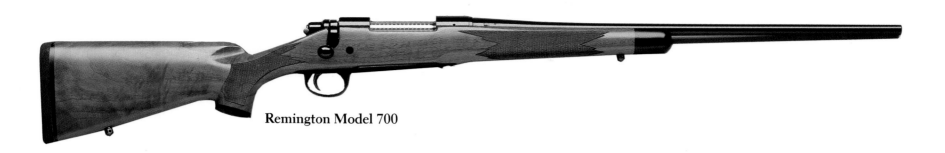

Remington Model 700

the great mechanical power of the turn bolt for extraction, and its one-piece stock and strong lockup that yields superb accuracy. Added to this is the more subtle fact that unlike the other actions, the bolt-action can be readily messed with and modified to suit the owner's taste. The trigger can easily be changed and the pull adjusted; the sights can be altered endlessly; the stock can be modified or simply replaced at will. And the handloader can have a ball developing the perfect load for his favorite rifle.

Today there are literally dozens of fine bolt-action hunting rifles on the market. These range from heavy-barreled varmint rifles to light sporters to large-caliber charge-stoppers—and everything in between. There are reasons, good ones, for choosing any of the other action types. But there is simply no hunting purpose for which a variety of bolt-actions aren't perfectly suited.

Because of its accuracy and reliability, the bolt-action is the odds-on choice for custom rifle

makers. Today the finest custom rifle makers in the world are American, and the rifles coming from their shops are things of beauty as well as utility—true works of art. The vast majority of these fine pieces are bolt-actions.

Sights

Without question, the telescopic sight, or riflescope, is the most popular today—and for good reason. You shoot better if you see better, and everyone sees better through a scope. Magnification is one reason but two other factors are also important. First, the scope puts the sight and the target in the same focal plane. With older iron sights, the eye must attempt to focus on rear sight, front sight, and target all at once—an impossibility. Something will be fuzzy, and the older one gets, the more pronounced the problem will become. The scope eliminates this problem; all one has to do is superimpose the scope's reticle (the cross hairs or post)

The bolt action has become the most popular hunting rifle action by far, available in virtually any imaginable configuration and chambered for cartridges suitable for any game on earth. Above is a lightweight over-the-counter Remington Model 700 Mountain rifle, while the rifle opposite is a one-of-a-kind custom .458 by gunmaker David Miller—truly the epitome of the gunmaker's art.

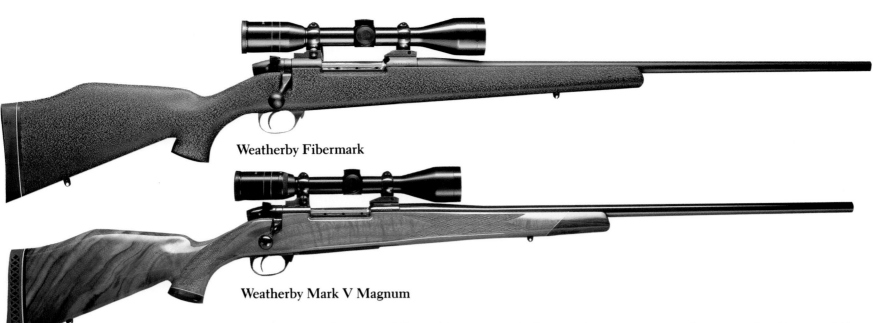

Weatherby Fibermark

Weatherby Mark V Magnum

on the target. Of equal importance is the scope's ability to gather available light. With a good scope you can see better in dim light than with the naked eye, which is very useful, because the murky dawn and dusk periods are critical in almost any hunting. The only application in which an iron sight is superior to a scope is in rain, for raindrops quickly obscure a scope's lenses. Some drawbacks to scopes are the hunter's fault. Too many hunters make the mistake of choosing a scope with too much magnification, making it useless at close range. For most hunting purposes a scope of $4\times$ is ideal, while in very open country a $6\times$ might be desirable. The most popular scopes today are variables, 2–$7\times$, 3–$9\times$, and so on. These are extremely useful, but hunters simply must remember to keep them at a lower power setting, no more than $4\times$, unless a longer shot calls for more magnification.

Today's scopes rarely fail—but scope mounts often do, usually due to poor mounting procedures. When mounting a scope, follow the directions carefully and use Loc-Tite on all screws. Properly

mounted, a scope should never shift zero and indeed will be more rugged than many of today's factory-supplied iron sights.

Hunting Handguns

Handgun hunting is a growing sport in America, with more and more states allowing handguns for big game all the time. The traditional hunting handgun has been a large-caliber revolver, generally a .41 or .44 Magnum. Either caliber is effective on deer-size game at relatively close range.

Today, in answer to handgunners' demands, there exists a whole class of specialty pistols designed for handgun hunting. Some of these are single shots, like Thompson/Center's Contender or Remington's XP100, chambered to cartridges traditionally thought of as rifle cartridges. Others are ultra-powerful revolvers, like the .454 Casull. No handgun can offer the potential power of a rifle; the short barrel and recoil limitations preclude that. But in skilled hands these specialty pistols

Remington XP-100

Handguns for hunters fall into two different categories: pistols packed along for such casual use as small game hunting and target practice and pistols designed for use as the primary hunting arm. A good .22 revolver like this classic High Standard, below, is an ideal camp gun. Remington's unique XP-100 bolt-action pistol, left, is chambered in cartridges for both varminting and big game hunting and is one of the world's most accurate firearms.

have been used to take virtually every game animal in the world, and handgun hunters enjoy the added challenge immensely.

As is the case with rifles, hunting handguns are vastly more efficient when scoped. Most scope manufacturers offer "long eye-relief" scopes for handgunners, meaning that the full field of view will be obtained when the scope is at arm's length. However, a scoped pistol simply must be shot from a rest. For close-range, close-cover work, an open-sighted handgun is thus superior to a scoped hand-gun—but the range must be kept short.

© Michael Havelin

Black-Powder Arms

Hunting with muzzleloaders is a popular sport today, and many states offer special muzzleloader seasons for modern "buckskinners." Modern replicas of Kentucky, Pennsylvania, and Hawken rifles are readily available, and there are several "modern muzzleloader" designs, some of which use a modern large-rifle primer for ignition instead of flint or a percussion cap. Whatever arm is chosen, today's muzzleloaders are extremely accurate, and hunting with them provides a most enjoyable nostalgic experience.

Most blackpowder hunters agree that .45 caliber is the absolute minimum for deer, while .50- to .54-caliber rifles are needed for larger game. In all cases, conical bullets are more effective than the traditional round balls—however, some guns are rifled to stabilize round balls rather than conicals; most guns will shoot one but not the other.

Two considerations are very important with blackpowder hunting. First, *practice*. That one shot is all that's available, so thorough knowledge of the rifle's capabilities is essential. Also, practice loading procedures endlessly. Sometimes a second shot, if delivered quickly enough, can prevent a long tracking job on a wounded animal. Second, be aware that wet weather is a real problem for a black-powder gun, almost hopeless for flintlock, and slightly less so for percussion.

Bowhunting Gear

Modern bowhunting is such a highly developed sport as to be almost an entirely separate subject. The modern compound bow is indeed a complex and most precise instrument, and it can be messed with and modified endlessly—perhaps more than even a bolt-action rifle.

Bowhunters are a very large group today, and indeed a large percentage of gun hunters bowhunt at least some of the time. And well they should, for bowhunters enjoy long seasons in most parts of the country. And they can hunt species such as elk and deer during the rut in many more areas than can rifle hunters.

There is growing controversy between "traditional" archers—those who use bare-limb longbows or recurves—and those who use the modern equipment, compound bows with sights, stabilizers, and such. This is unfortunate, for bowhunting itself has become the target of anti-hunting groups, and in this day and age, all hunters need to stick together.

Regardless of one's choice of equipment, proficiency is the key to successful bowhunting—even more than with firearms. The serious bowhunter simply must make a commitment to practice extensively; the best archers shoot some amount *every day!* There is no question that a properly sharpened broadhead in the right place is deadly and efficient. The key is getting it in the right place, which is no

different than with the rifle hunter and his bullet. The difference is that it takes much more skill for the bowhunter to place his arrow properly. Of course, it's that added challenge that's the spice of the bowhunter's life.

Modern bowhunting tackle has come a long way from the days of the longbow; the modern hunting bow is indeed a complex instrument. Technology has made the bow more effective—but not necessarily easier to shoot. Successful bowhunting requires a serious commitment to regular shooting practice—far more than is required with a rifle.

Clothing and Equipment

The world has become high tech, and the seemingly old-fashioned sport of hunting hasn't escaped the changes. There's so much gear and gadgetry, and so many goodies available to today's hunter that it's a wonder we aren't too loaded down to move when we head afield. And that's the pitfall. As with hunting arms, technology is wonderful, but it provides no substitute for hunting skill and patience. On the other hand, the hunter's gear today is better than ever. Provided he has basic hunting skills, patience, and a bit of luck, he's likely to be successful—and whether he is or not, his hours afield can be even more enjoyable than ever.

Hunting Optics

While optics are important in relatively few bird-hunting situations, good binoculars are the big-game hunter's right hand. In fact, after the rifle itself, most serious big-game hunters rate binoculars the most important piece of gear. My old friend Jack Atcheson, Jr., the Butte, Montana, booking agent and sheep outfitter, somewhat ironically claims that binoculars are so important that they "cost nothing and weigh nothing."

This is saying a lot, for in fact, the best binoculars cost a very great deal—but they're worth it,

The importance of optics in nearly all forms of hunting simply can't be stressed enough. Often considered tools best-suited to high mountains or open plains, binoculars are every bit as useful in the deep woods for picking game out of the natural camouflage.

and with binoculars, even more than with firearms, you absolutely get what you pay for. A good pair of binoculars saves an untold amount of walking—and prevents a hunter from bypassing who knows how much game by mistake.

In relatively open country, glassing, or carefully surveying the area, with binoculars is a hunting technique in and of itself. Depending on the type of country, the best choice of optics might be 7, 8, or 10 × binoculars—or perhaps in very big country, 15 × binoculars mounted on a tripod. The idea is to sit down, get comfortable, and literally dismantle the countryside piece by piece.

The first key to the success of this method is to know, through scouting or research, that you're in good game country. The second key is to believe that if you look hard enough and long enough you'll see what you're looking for—and have the patience and faith to stay at it until you do. This can mean long hours of glassing, and poor-quality binoculars will quickly reveal themselves through headaches and eye strain.

With other types of big-game hunting—stand hunting, still hunting in heavy cover—binoculars aren't used so extensively. Rather, they're just used to scan the cover ahead (usually a relatively short distance) before moving. Or, from a stand, binoc-

© Craig Boddington

In big country, above, a good, clear spotting scope saves countless miles of tough walking. Binoculars are used to actually spot the game, but a spotting scope is the answer for determining if horns or antlers are worth a closer look. Opposite: These binoculars by Swarovski, top, and Nikon are good examples of mid-size roof-prism glasses. In 8X magnification and rubber-armored, both are excellent all-around hunting binoculars.

© Dick Thomas/Visuals Unlimited

Binoculars and riflescope, above, are two pieces of gear no mountain hunter would leave camp without, but a third piece of "optics" that can be even more important is a good compass. The western mountains, opposite, offer beautiful hunting country, but the distances are vast. Powerful riflescopes can't and don't make up for stalking skills, but even so, western shooting averages a good deal longer than in the eastern timber, so variable-power scopes are a sensible option.

ulars are used to scan the brush at the limits of your vision. Admittedly, it is not critical to have the highest-quality binoculars for this more casual use. However, besides the clarity of image and alignment of lenses that prevent eye strain, top-quality binoculars have another benefit. They will gather more of the available light than inexpensive glasses, thus allowing you to see better during the critical early-morning and late-evening periods.

The current rage in binoculars is toward shirt-pocket-size "minis." Like full-size glasses, these run the full gamut of quality and price. For still hunting in heavy cover or to use on a final stalk, they're just fine. However, beware of using them when serious glassing is called for. They cannot gather light like full-size binoculars, nor are they as comfortable when you have to hold them steady during lengthy glassing sessions.

Endless discussion could be held on the advantages of roof-prism (straight-tubed) binoculars versus the Porro-prism (offset lenses) binoculars and between individual-eyepiece focus versus center focus. I prefer the "feel" of the Porro-prism glasses for prolonged glassing, and I prefer the ease of center focus. But the roof-prism models are more compact, and in theory, individual-eyepiece focusing allows for more precise adjustment. So long as you purchase a good pair, I think whatever pleases you is the best. I do prefer rubber-armored models, not only to protect the glasses but also so they

won't clang around as much when you are stalking game and need to be quiet.

What's a good make? There are many good types, from Germany, Austria, Japan, and the United States. It's hard to get a really good pair of binoculars for less than the cost of a rifle, but some less expensive binoculars are very good buys. The best course is to go to a dealer who has a wide selection and really compare the various models. Take your time, because binoculars are a serious purchase that will last for many years.

In really open country or high mountains it makes good sense to back up your binoculars with a spotting scope. There are many good ones that are reasonably compact. I've always gotten good service from a fixed 20 or 25 × glass, but variables with magnification up to 36 × can be useful. In the field, though, the very powerful scopes have the problem of mirage, and they must be absolutely steady—which is tough on a windy mountainside. A sturdy little tripod with rubber cups on the legs is essential; you just can't get steady enough without one. With spotting scopes it isn't nearly so essential to buy the best, although when you're trying to count points on a buck at 2,000 yards, every bit of optical clarity you can get is needed. And if you can't see the points, you'll have to walk over there for a closer look. That's why Jack Atcheson, Jr., says optics "cost nothing and weigh nothing." He's right!

© Sharon Cummings/Dembinsky Photo Associates

Packs

Hunters always have gear to carry, whether they're just going out for a morning's hunt or an extended backpack trip. But there's another primary reason to have a pack: to carry game out after you've had a successful hunt.

If you're hunting reasonably close to your horse or vehicle, you aren't too worried about the second requirement. But if you're hunting in remote country far from roads, you'd better worry about it!

Here's a look at good packs for casual hunting. What you need really depends on how much you have to carry. Fanny packs are extremely popular these days; you'll find them in any and all fabrics and camouflage patterns. They're comfortable, but don't hold very much. If all you need is a sandwich and flashlight and perhaps a light rain jacket rolled up tight and tied on, a fanny pack will do you just fine. If you're like me and carry a camera and perhaps a long lens, a spotting scope with a tripod, plus all the normal gear, there's no fanny pack that will do the job. Instead I carry a day pack—and these, too, are available in any fabric, color, or camouflage pattern you can imagine.

I have a green canvas day pack from Roosevelt, and it's very simple—teardrop shaped, one roomy inner pocket, and one outer pocket, with well-padded straps—but there are several things I like about it. First off, it's waterproof—which is the single most important requirement if you carry

© Craig Boddington

It's important to always have a plan for getting your game out of the field if you're successful—and that plan can include horses, opposite, or a packframe, left. Remember that if any distance must be covered on foot, carrying even a fairly heavy load like this whole pronghorn buck is much easier than dragging it, but keep in mind how much you can carry and how far.

The Hunter's Day Pack

It's all too easy to load yourself up with unnecessary gear, but there are certain items that should go in your day pack or fanny pack whenever you leave camp. Although you'll want to make adjustments depending on the weather, terrain, and what you're hunting for, here's my personal checklist:

extra ammunition
matches *and* butane lighter
fire starter (small squares of inner-tube rubber)
compass
knife
sharpening steel
space blanket
nylon twine
full canteen
first-aid kit
Krazy Glue
duct tape
rain suit
flashlight with extra bulbs and batteries
spotting scope
tripod
camera with flash, film, and spare batteries
for heavy game: saw, game hoist

cameras afield. That's a real problem with the polar-fleece day packs so popular right now. Second, it's reasonably quiet. Not as quiet as polar fleece, but certainly more quiet than Cordura. Finally, it's comfortable—something you can only find out after carrying a bag for a while.

But a day pack is just that, a day pack. It won't carry your camp, nor will it carry your game out. For those chores I've tried packs of all types, and depending on the load, there's a wide variety that will work. But when loads get heavy—whether it's a backpack hunt or a matter of packing out large animals some distance—there's no substitute for a good pack frame.

There are two types: The older, external frame, with or without a packsack, and the much newer, internal-frame packs. The Camp Trails Freighter, with or without packsack, is the classic hunter's pack frame. Internal-frame packs, which are marvelously comfortable, are the latest with serious mountain climbers, and thus sheep hunters are adopting them as well.

Again, comfort is the key issue, plus a knowledge of how much you can carry in safety, without hurting yourself and being pulled too badly off balance. I have a small Coleman Peak 1 space-age plastic frame that I use for packing smaller deer, but for big deer and quarters of larger game, I prefer a Camp Trails Freighter.

Whatever you prefer, there is no substitute for a good load-carrying device. In fact, packing game is incomparably easier than dragging it! *But* you must know how much you can carry and how far you can carry it. If the backpack is your means of getting your game out, that distance is the hunting limit that you must not exceed.

In almost universal use throughout North American hunting country, the classic backpacking hunter's packframe is the Camp Trails Freighter. Camp Trails offers a variety of packsacks in different configurations and colors, including these camouflage versions.

Knives

The hunting knife is a pretty basic hunter's tool, but you're in a real mess if you leave it at home! Knives, like guns, range from very plain to very ornate, but most will get the job done.

I like both fixed blades and folders, with no particular preference for either. However, if a folding-blade knife is chosen, it simply must have a blade lock. During the field-dressing chores, it's necessary to work by feel inside the body cavity while severing the windpipe and cutting the diaphragm. A knife without a blade lock is simply asking for trouble.

Blade shape and length is a matter of personal preference, but generally a blade exceeding four inches in length is harder to control. The traditional general-purpose knife blade is called a clip pattern: straight blade, slight curve to the point, spine straight for about two-thirds, then curving down and rising to the point. Such a blade has more point than you really need for skinning and field-dressing, and that point can have a bad habit of cutting things you don't want cut. Better, to my way of thinking, is the drop-point or centered-point pattern, where the tip of a fairly broad blade has a more sweeping curve and the spine drops gently to meet an almost-rounded point.

Whatever blade shape is chosen, of equal importance is that the blade be able to take and hold an edge, and that you carry in your day pack or fanny

© Tony Mandile

Hunters are pretty much evenly divided today between traditional fixed-blade knives like these and more compact folders. Whichever is preferred, most hunters agree that a knife with a blade much in excess of four inches is unwieldly for field-dressing and skinning chores. Blade shape is very much a matter of personal preference, but the quality of the steel and its ability to take and hold an edge are of paramount importance.

Buck Knives of El Cajon, California, started the trend toward folders many years ago with their Folding Hunter, a knife that made Buck a household word. Today's lineup includes both the Folding Hunter and slightly smaller Ranger, both shown in Finger Groove models. These knives feature the popular general-purpose clip-pattern blade and have sturdy blade locks.

pack the means for keeping it sharp. All too many knives today are made of steel that's very hard and difficult to sharpen. And most stainless steel blades are also hard to sharpen, requiring diamond-impregnated whetstones.

I carry a sharpening steel for touching up the edge, and I often touch up a blade while I'm working with game. A quick way to get into trouble is to allow the blade to become very dull before you sharpen it. Then, when you do, you have a radical difference in the cutting properties, and it will get away from you.

The handle design is also important. It must have a comfortable, hand-fitting grip, and it's best if the handle material gives a solid feel and plenty of controllability. Stag antler handles are traditional, and the rough surface offers a good, positive grip even when wet and slippery. Even better are some of the modern synthetic materials, Kraton and such, that offer a good grip under the worst conditions.

All too many hunts come to a disastrous end when a knife slips—and, miles from anywhere, that can be a serious problem. Common sense should apply—don't get in a hurry, always cut away from yourself, and don't allow your hands to become too cold and clumsy. The last time I cut myself was in sub-zero cold in the high Arctic; I simply got in a hurry while field-dressing a musk-ox.

A knife will perform all the field-dressing chores, and with a bit of skill, it's possible to quarter even the largest animal with a knife alone. However, a bone saw is a fine gadget to have and will save time. There are many good lightweight hunters' saws on the market, and for hunting very large game, one should be included as part of the kit.

Hunting Clothing

Outdoor clothing has become not only high tech, but high fashion as well. And this proliferation of outstanding outdoor wear is good news for hunters. In the "good old days," hunters stayed warm with wool or down-insulated clothing and dry with rubberized rain gear.

Wool is still good stuff, make no mistake about that. It's quiet and retains its warmth when wet. It also breathes quite well. But, unfortunately, wool is heavy and soaks up water like a sponge. Down-filled garments, also good stuff indeed, have the major drawback of losing warmth very quickly when wet—and, like wool, down dries very slowly.

Rubberized rainsuits are among the most waterproof garments around to this day and reasonably windproof as well—but they don't breathe at all, making them extremely uncomfortable to walk in.

Today there are a number of synthetic fibers, fabrics, and films that offer sound alternatives to these tried-and-true products. Insulators such as Holofill and Thinsulate have largely replaced down in outerwear, and they're marvelous—lighter and every bit as warm, even when wet.

If there's a problem with the new insulators, it's that they've often been put inside Cordura nylon outer shells. Cordura is as tough as nails, but it's extremely noisy, scratching terribly against brush and leaves. Recognizing this, the manufacturers have responded with Cordura/Supplex blends—one

© Chuck Schmeiser/Unicorn Stock Photos

What Do Deer See?

In the past we've always believed that deer and other big-game species saw their world in black and white only. New research indicates that most animals' color vision is indeed limited—but not totally absent. It is now believed that animals see shades of violet, blue, green, and yellow, but are unable to distinguish red as a color.

Perhaps more important, animals see into the ultraviolet spectrum, whereas humans cannot. This is critical because many household detergents contain ultraviolet brighteners, which, to human eyes, give that "whiter than white" effect. To animals, especially in the early morning and late evening when ultraviolet light is most active, this may actually be seen as a glow of reflected UV light—much like what we see under a black light. Many clothing dyes, too, even those with which camouflage clothing is dyed, used to contain UV brighteners, thus, perhaps, making hunters "glow" to their quarry. Hunting-clothes manufacturers have lately been seeking out dyes without UV brighteners. One company, Atsko/Sno-Seal, markets UV-Killer, a treatment that removes ultraviolet fluorescence. Much research remains to be done on the subject, but it seems to answer the question every hunter has about the deer that spotted him when he was motionless in good camouflage!

© Will Brewster

The incredible proliferation of hunting outerwear enables today's hunters to be more comfortable—and more fashionable, as shown above— than ever before. As good as the modern clothing is, however, most Arctic hunters, top right, have learned that it doesn't beat the traditional Eskimo caribou-skin clothing. Fortunately most hunting takes place in somewhat more temperate climate. The TreBark camouflage pattern, bottom right, one of many of today's "proprietary" designs, is ideal in the eastern turkey woods.

such brand is "Quiet Cloth." This is progress, but bowhunters and still hunters will still find such products too noisy.

Synthetic fleece, with Polarfleece being the most familiar trade name, is the answer for quiet. Soft, reasonably warm, and quick drying, fleece is the modern bow hunter's answer in cool weather. One problem fleece does have that prospective users must beware of: It is not windproof in the least! For quiet wear in cold, windy country, traditional wool remains the best answer.

In the world of keeping dry, there are two totally divergent technologies sweeping North America today. One, the high-tech path, is characterized by Gore-Tex. Not a fabric itself, but a film laminated to fabric, Gore-Tex is totally waterproof yet absolutely breathable—and surprisingly windproof as well. The problem with Gore-Tex is properly sealing the seams, a manufacturing problem that gave Gore-Tex a bad name in its first few years. That problem is solved now: If a garment has a hang tag stating the approval of the W.L. Gore company, then the seams have been properly sealed and the garment can be expected to be waterproof.

If any problem remains with Gore-Tex, it's that nagging difficulty of it not being quite quiet enough for close-cover hunting. The Gore-Tex film itself has a slight rustle to it, and in the past, this was compounded by bonding it to noisy fabric such as Cordura. Today Gore-Tex is bonded to Supplex,

Polarfleece, and even wool and wool blends, which reduces the noise significantly. Gore-Tex, together with similar products just now coming out, is without question the best waterproofing for the wilderness hunter, offering light weight and versatility.

The other new rain gear option is new only in the United States. That's the waxed or oiled cotton so popular in Europe for generations, the outerwear typified by England's Barbour. The waxed cotton is marvelously waterproof, reasonably breathable, and gets very quiet with age. Unfortunately it's far too heavy to be considered for wilderness hunting on foot. It is a very sound option for stand hunters, still hunters close to home, and bird hunters.

Underwear, too, has gone high tech. While the older waffle-weave cotton and cotton-wool blends remain warm and comfortable, better still are new synthetics that do a much better job of wicking perspiration away from the body. Polypropylene is one such synthetic long underwear. Thermax from DuPont is another. Both are also available in socks, face masks, and gloves—good bases to build your wardrobe on top of.

While modern fabrics have made a huge difference in the hunter's attire, so has the proliferation of camouflage patterns. The World War II woodland camo pattern was perhaps the first camouflage widely used by hunters, and it's still around. But in the past decade, there have been literally dozens of

The Layered Approach

Most types of hunting involve a combination of moving and sitting. Staying warm while moving isn't a problem, especially in rough country. The problem comes when you sweat and then stop to glass or sit for a while. Layering, or wearing several layers of clothing so that as you warm up with exercise you can remove outer layers to prevent perspiring unduly, is the only sensible approach. Here are a couple of examples.

In *extremely* cold weather, approaching zero degrees Fahrenheit or just below freezing with significant wind chill, start with Thermax long underwear next to the skin. Add on wool trousers and heavy wool shirt, with down or Hollofill vest on top; silk scarf around neck; ski mask and knit wool cap (big enough to cover ears); thermax gloves; two pairs of heavy socks, wool or Thermax, the outer pair wader socks up to the knees; and insulated boots, felt-lined pacs if in snow. This ensemble works well while moving, but in the day pack I'd carry a Gore-Tex suit and Thinsulate gloves to put on when sitting still.

If it is above freezing but you expect a wind-chill factor, I'd start with silk or other lightweight long underwear. On top would be heavy jeans or light wool trousers, Worsterlon (a flannel-like synthetic that dries very quickly) shirt, Thermax gloves, silk scarf, cap with ear flaps, and down or Hollofill vest—probably worn open while walking. Footwear would depend on terrain, but would be worn over one light pair and one heavy pair of socks. In my day pack would be a Gore-Tex suit, specifically Remington's Ultimate Climate Suit, Thinsulate gloves, and a ski mask.

proprietary patterns springing up all over the country. Some are very versatile, while others are best suited for a particular kind of vegetation or background. None is necessarily better than any other, for all serve to break up the human outline and form. Just a few of today's popular patterns are TreBark, RealTree, Hide-'n-Pine, Mossy Oak, ASAT (All Season All Terrain), Bushlan, and, well, the list goes on.

The primary users of camouflage are bowhunters and spring turkey hunters, because rifle hunters are required to wear blaze orange in more and more states. Of course, blaze is also available in camo patterns that break up the human form. While I have little doubt that a deer can see a brilliant blaze orange garment—if not as a color, then certainly as something out of place—I have come

Many types of hunting require uneven levels of exertion—some combination of rapid movement, sitting still, and slow movement. Therefore, the layered approach is the most sensible method of dressing: layers of outer clothing that can be removed when walking and put back on when sitting still. The trick is to keep from sweating heavily when moving, because at lower temperatures that perspiration can literally turn to ice when you stop.

to take great comfort in its brightness in the deer woods, especially on public land. In some states, once you're in a tree stand you can take it off, but whether it's required or not, I recommend at least a blaze orange hat at all times; it's a good piece of insurance against other hunters mistaking you for game.

Boots

Cordura and Gore-Tex have wrought the biggest changes in hunting boots. Rare today is the boot made wholly of leather; instead, tough Cordura panels reduce weight without affecting durability. Gore-Tex makes boots more waterproof than ever before. The old problem with seam sealing was more prevalent in boots than in outerwear, but that has been solved in recent years. Today's Gore-Tex boots from reliable makers are indeed waterproof—and lighter than ever. Insulated boots today are likely to have Thinsulate insulation, for compact, lightweight, and warm insulation.

Vibram soles took the world by storm a number of years ago, and they're still good. But today the newest lug sole is called Air Bob, and it offers almost as much traction as the Vibram lug, without picking up as much ice and mud.

Overall, the trend among walking hunters is toward lighter and lighter-weight boots. For truly cold weather, space-age boots insulated with closed-cell foam keep hunters warmer than ever before—and that's perhaps the best news of all!

Gun Gear to Take Along

Any time you travel any distance at all to hunt—especially if you'll be gone more than a day or two—there are some basic "emergency" gun items that should go along.

First and foremost is a cleaning rod that will fit your rifle, pistol, or shotgun bore. Not because it's so critical that your firearm be cleaned on the hunt, but, rather, so you can clear the bore if you happen to take a spill and get some foreign matter down there. One way to prevent this from happening is to carry along a roll of good plastic tape. Especially in wet or snowy weather savvy hunters often put a strip of tape over the muzzle at the start of each hunting day. It will not affect pressure, velocity, or accuracy in any way, but will prevent gunk from getting down the muzzle.

With the cleaning rod should go oil, cleaning solvent, and some rags or patching material so that in the event of a long, wet day, you can clean your firearm before rust forms. You should also have screwdrivers that will fit the screws on your gun so you can take it apart for thorough cleaning and oiling if needed.

Don't forget the little things—scope caps, sling, extra ammo. Commercial scope caps are fine, but a handy cover can also be made by cutting a rubber band–shaped circular piece from an old inner tube. It will fit tight but can be removed instantly—just pull up on one end and turn loose.

Slings, though noisy in heavy cover, are not only handy for carrying the rifle, they're even more valuable as an aid to steady shooting. Learn how to use a "hasty sling" when shooting offhand, kneeling, or sitting—you'll be amazed at what a difference it makes!

Birds and Bird Dogs

Dad had a huge Irish setter when I was young. Old Timmy was a gentle dog, and I learned to walk by wrapping my arms around his red neck and placing my feet on his front pads. Tim was a real hunting setter, one of the last of his kind; the field savvy of Irish setters was bred out of them in the recent past in favor of the show strains. Dad and my grandfather would take old Timmy up through Nebraska to South Dakota and from one end of our own Kansas to the other—and I dreamed of the day when I could go along.

It wasn't to be; by the time I was big enough to go, the old setter was gone—and it wasn't until I was nearly grown that I had the opportunity to really understand about birds and bird dogs. When I grew old enough to learn to hunt, Dad was still between bird dogs, in that long period when you want a dog but know you'll never have another like the one you've lost, and thus are reluctant to try. We hunted those Kansas quail and pheasants, for sure—the hard way, acting as our own bird dogs. Perhaps it was well that we did, for I learned early the most likely covers to find game. Undoubtedly I became a better shot, for I learned to shoot birds when their flush was always a surprise rather the expected climax to a staunch point.

Eventually we had bird dogs—a succession of canine maniacs that proved conclusively the Irish setter was now a show, rather than field, breed. Proved, too, that a poor bird dog is far worse than none at all. And then, in an unprecedented break from our beloved red setters, we had Sam. I had gotten parental approval to keep a bird dog, a real one, such approval being absolutely essential since I'd soon be off to college fifty miles away. So the talent search began.

For the waterfowl hunter, few sights are as stirring as the sight of a skein of Canada geese, left. Although drought and loss of wetland habitat have reduced duck populations in most flyways, North America's goose numbers today are at what may be an all-time high.

Waterfowl hunting can be accomplished without the aid of a dog, but a well-trained retriever makes retrieving downed birds immeasurably easier. And as in all bird hunting with a dog, half the fun of the hunt is watching a good dog at work.

I found Sam, perhaps eighteen months old, bedraggled and forlorn, tied under a trailer not far from the trap range where much of my misspent youth was misspent. He was supposed to be an English setter and probably could have been papered as a purebred if anyone cared. He had fear in his manner and a ridiculous rat tail, but a broad, square head and intelligent eyes. Dave Bledsoe, owner of good setters and the finest quail shot I ever knew, was with me, and he said we should give the dog a try. So I paid the man thirty-five dollars, and we drove off with my new dog.

His previous owner said he'd been worked a bit; quite possibly he had been. But not very much, for nobody with an inkling of what that dog could do would turn him loose for the price of a few weeks' dog food. We took him out behind the trap range, where I knew a semi-tame covey of birds could be found. He was frightened and unsure; I petted him a bit, then headed him toward a brushy pond dike and unsnapped his leash, not knowing whether I'd ever see him again.

He ran wild for a few minutes, and I hollered and chased him down. Then we started again, into

© Hanson Carroll/FPG International

Dog Care Afield

A good bird dog enjoys the hunt every bit as much as you do, but he needs your help to maintain peak performance. First and foremost is water. To keep your dog healthy, as well as to keep him active and his nose in good working order, you must make sure he has water frequently—in warmer weather, at least every hour or so. If you're hunting in dry country with no streams or ponds, carry a canteen and plastic dish in your game bag. Many gun dogs will not eat while they're working, but carry along some high-energy dog snacks as well just in case. Even a portion of your peanut-butter-and-jelly sandwich will give a dog a burst of energy.

Thorns are always a potential problem, more so in some areas than others, and barbed wire also poses a genuine hazard. Carry along needle-nose pliers to extract thorns, and have some antiseptic and bandages in the car in case your dog (or you!) runs into a real problem.

Regardless of the level of training of your dog, you should always carry a leash or at least some cord that will serve as one in a pinch. You may need to lead your four-footed friend away from another dog, a stray cat, or who knows what.

Remember that your dog will be exerting far more energy than you. Watch closely for signs of exhaustion, heat stroke in hot weather, and hypothermia in cold weather. Most gun dogs will give their all for their masters, so make certain you aren't asking too much!

the breeze, and he hit scent he was born understanding. He hesitated, then locked up tight. Not classic; that rat tail was too low, and he was off balance and had to correct. He broke point, too, when I walked in and put the small covey up. We could work on the details, and we would—but what he had from birth a thousand years of the best trainers couldn't give him. Bledsoe grunted, "Well, boy, looks like you got yourself a bird dog."

Indeed I did, and thanks to Sam the next several autumns held the finest bird shooting any hunter could imagine. With maturity and better care, that

rat tail grew to a luxurious plume of silky feathers, and he held it low only for singles and uncertain finds. On a covey or the strong scent of a rooster pheasant, that tail would be high and proud, and there would be no mistake.

Sam wasn't perfect; no dog or man is. He had the best nose I've seen before or since, and his points were as stylish as any field-trial champion's. We could start down a mile-long hedgerow with Sammy running hell-for-leather in front of us. If he came back, we'd find another hedgerow. If he didn't, we knew we'd find him up ahead, locked

© Will Brewster

up solid. But I was young and impatient, and Sam followed my lead. He would find dead birds readily; with that long nose, it was puppy play. But retrieving wasn't his thing. He could do it, but he didn't like it; he'd rather get on with it and find more birds. And I allowed that to be his big failing.

We hunted alone a lot, a good team. And often with Dave Bledsoe and his big male setter Bowser and petite, stylish little Belle. In the car together, Sam and Bowser would fight, always—but in the field, all business, with each dog honoring the other's points like perfect gentlemen. Word got out about Sam, and I discovered that a hunter with a good dog isn't short on invitations!

Sam's been gone a long time now. He was good till the end, in spite of a melon-size tumor that was removed. Neither Dad nor I have had another setter, red *or* white, since. I have a wonderful springer spaniel now—a good retriever, this one. Flushing dogs are much better suited to the running western quail I hunt now in California's foothills. But even if bobwhite quail were still my local game, I'm not sure I could have another setter. Few of us are privileged to have more than one really great bird dog in our lifetimes, and I've had mine.

To the serious waterfowler, which I have never been, a great bird dog would undoubtedly be a retrieving breed. To a grouse hunter in the upper

© Hanson Carroll/FPG International

experience with birds. And then there's the element of luck: putting these ingredients together at the right time and place. For without good training and plenty of experience, a dog with the best bloodlines in the world will never become great. Nor can the world's best professional trainer turn a dog into a bird dog without the native instincts and senses. And without the opportunity to use those instincts and training—use them extensively and as a young dog—there is no hope for greatness.

These fortunate circumstances will come together infrequently, but when they do, and you have such a dog, cherish the moments and enjoy them. They're fleeting, for a man will outlive his dog, and if a dog is great, his like won't be seen again soon. But you will learn great truths from such a dog, and they will last throughout your life. You'll learn that the classic forms of bird hunting, whether upland or waterfowl, indeed provide some of the most enjoyable hours afield. But those hours are so much better spent watching a great dog do his work than spent alone that the dog's work will become as important as the shooting of the birds. And when it's your own dog, the experience is all the more sweet.

When you have had a great dog, but no longer do, only then will you truly understand the degree to which birds and bird dogs go together.

It takes extensive training and lots of experience to turn a puppy into a finished gun dog. But natural talent—inbred hunting instincts—are an all-important third ingredient that simply must be present. This pup, facing page, shows the interest you want to see. Left, the springer spaniel, a flushing breed, is a fine choice for a grouse dog.

Midwest, it might be a close-working springer. The hunter who pursues a variety of birds with equal zest might prefer a German shorthair. For me, in the endless hedgerows of my native Kansas, the perfect bird dog would be a big-running pointer or setter.

Whatever your favorite type of bird hunting, and whatever your favorite breed of dog, having a really great canine hunting companion is largely a combination of the dog's breeding, good training, and the opportunity for your dog to gain a lot of

Upland Birds

North America is blessed with an incredible diversity of upland birds, both native and introduced. We have fully a half dozen species of quail, as many and more of grouse, plus our naturalized citizens: pheasant, Hungarian partridge, and chukar. And then there are the technically migratory doves, wild pigeons, and woodcock. Though we speak of all these collectively as "upland game," the hunting of them is as enormously varied as the diverse habitats in which they are found. We'll briefly examine the dogs, guns, and hunting tactics for America's upland game.

© John Gerlach/Dembinsky Photo Associates

Quail

The bobwhite is America's best-known quail, a bird that thrives in the edge habitat of the Deep South and Midwest to the foothills of the Rockies. But he's hardly our only quail; in Texas the blue quail takes over, giving way to the Gambel's quail of the Arizona deserts. Along the Pacific coast are found the California valley quail, and in high country above, the big, plump mountain quail. Rounding out America's quail are the little-known Mearn's quail of the rugged mountains along Arizona's and New Mexico's border with Mexico.

The bobwhite is the gentleman's bird. Found in coveys of a dozen to, rarely, thirty birds, he holds well for pointing dogs both on covey finds and singles. Throughout the South, "bird" means bobwhite quail and is so understood by all hunters.

Traditionally bobwhite quail are hunted along the edges of cultivation using big-running pointing dogs, English pointers or setters being the most popular. Since the birds hold well, shots are close; open-chokes and number 7½ shot are favored, and experienced gunners do extremely well with small gauges.

Bobwhite hunting without dogs is very difficult and not nearly as productive, but can be done by a couple of hunters slowly working small strips of cover—brushy fencerows, creek bottoms, and such. An important key to locating birds is their "bobwhite" gathering call.

Today, with so much of the South going from cultivated lands to pine forest, much quail hunting is done in the woods—much more difficult shooting, and more difficult, too, to locate birds. Good dog work is ever more important in such non-traditional habitats.

A bobwhite's feathers blend in perfectly with fall ground cover, so finding downed birds without a dog is extremely difficult. Even with a good dog, it's extremely important to carefully mark the fall of a bird—and to never shoot a second bird, even if the opportunity arises, until you're certain you've got the first one pegged.

The little Mearn's quail of the Southwest's high grassy valleys holds even more tightly than the bob-white; the only chance to hunt them is with pointing dogs—and the more ground they cover, the better. But the rest of the western quail are hardly gentlemen. They're big runners, and they'll outrun a dog as well as a man. Trying to hunt them with pointing dogs is an exercise in futility for the hunters and frustration for their canine counterparts. Blue, also called scaled quail, and the scarce mountain quail run the most, but Gambel's and valley quail are nearly as bad.

The only chance to get good shooting, and even some good dog work, is to flush the coveys and break them up; single birds will hold a bit better. A flushing dog can do this, and so can a hunter, by charging the covey pell-mell. The other tactic, often

The sharptail grouse, far left, and Hungarian partridge, above, are popular gamebirds of the northern plains. The sharptail is a native grouse, about the size of a hen pheasant, while the fast-flying Hun is a successful import. Their ranges overlap in the Dakotas and eastern Montana, offering sporty mixed-bag gunning.

Hunting bobwhite quail over a staunch-pointing dog is a time-honored tradition in the South, where the bobwhite is simply called *bird*. The western species of quail are strong runners and tend not to hold as well for pointing dogs as the gentlemanly bobwhite. Far right, the willow ptarmigan of Canada and Alaska, a member of the grouse family, is a plentiful but little-hunted gamebird.

used on blue quail, is to try to shoot a sprinting bird on the ground. That sounds unsporting to bobwhite hunters, but it is one of the only ways to get a covey up and scattered before the birds just plain outdistance you.

In the typically open, arid habitat of Gambel and scaled quail, hunting without a dog is quite practical—and sometimes sensible, depending on the density of cactus. For all of these western birds, close-ranging dogs are essential. Brittanys, springers, and German shorthairs are popular, and many hunters use retrievers kept at heel for collecting downed birds. Even with close-ranging dogs, the shooting will be farther than with bobwhites, and it's important to hit these strong runners very hard. Modified-chokes are the most popular, and the 20-gauge is the minimum that should be used. Western quail are often located by calling.

Grouse

As "bird" means bobwhite to southerners, so "grouse" means ruffed grouse in the East and upper Midwest (though it is called "pa'tridge" in New England). Hunting the ruffed grouse is almost a religion among those who pursue the bird. Living in the heaviest cover—or "coverts," as they are called—the ruffed grouse presents some of the most difficult wingshooting in the world. Serious grouse hunters speak in terms of birds flushed or "moved"—never in terms of birds shot at, much less brought to bag!

Hunting ruffed grouse is a game for tightly controlled, close-working dogs, whether pointing or flushing breeds. Brittanys and springers are popular, but virtually all pointing and flushing breeds are used; the major requirement is that they work *close*. The classic grouse gun is a double-barrel, open of choke, short, and fast handling. For the shooting will indeed be fast and often at a bird obscured by limbs and brush.

But Old Ruff is hardly the last word in American grouse hunting. In fact, out West he's found in the forested regions and rarely hunted. They call him a "fool hen" and maintain you can hunt him with a stick. Instead, to a westerner "grouse" means prairie grouse: sharp-tails, sage grouse, or greater and lesser prairie chickens.

Found in the prairies, sagebrush flats, and foothills of the West, these birds live in large flocks in typically sparse ground cover. Big-running dogs will simply flush them wild, and indeed they don't hold well for pointing dogs at any distance. Westerners often hunt them by sight, or if they use dogs, they're most likely to use a retriever kept at heel. But a flushing dog, kept in close, can work them quite well.

In some cases, particularly with prairie chickens, the birds are actually hunted by pass shooting: staking out a known feeding field at first light, then shooting at the birds when they come whistling in to feed. Many hunters also hunt them with binoculars, locating flocks at long range before setting out on foot.

Distances are obviously much farther with western grouse, and the birds can be large. Sage grouse can be giant, weighing up to eight pounds. Modified chokes are the typical choice, and a 20-gauge loaded with high-velocity sixes is a good minimum for western grouse. Guns should be kept light, too, since walking up these western birds can require covering many miles!

Then there are the forest grouse of the West and Canada—spruce grouse, blue grouse, and way out there, even ruffed grouse. Hunted but little, these grouse are actually quite common in much of the western forests. The few westerners who pursue them do so in much the same fashion that easterners hunt ruffed grouse—but consider them a great deal easier to hunt!

Finally one must not forget the not one but three varieties of ptarmigan. In the Rockies, the ptarmigan is a high-country bird, but farther north, all across Canada and into Alaska, ptarmigan are exceedingly common. Outsiders usually pursue them as an adjunct to hunts for caribou, moose, and other northern species—either for sport or for the pot. These beautiful birds, which are snow white in winter, tend to hold close for pointing or flushing dogs and are marvelous sport. But their habitat is so remote that relatively few hunters pursue them for their own merits.

Game Care Tips for Birds

One of the biggest problems with game birds is that they're normally carried in a rubberized game bag next to your back, where their body heat can't escape and your own compounds the problem. Game bags are an unavoidable necessity in the field—the only option is a bird strap, which isn't practical in heavy brush. But get your birds out of the bag as quickly as possible, placing them either in a cooler or in open shade, where a breeze can help dissipate the body heat.

On warm days or especially with birds that have a reputation for strong flavor (such as sage grouse and spruce grouse), it's wise to eviscerate your birds as quickly as possible—preferably before you put them in the game bag to continue your hunt. Just make a small incision between the base of the breast and the tail and pull everything out.

© Sharon Cummings/Dembinsky Photo Associates

Imports

The ring-necked pheasant is one of America's most important game birds, so traditional a quarry that it's hard to remember that it was first brought to North America from Asia just a century ago. Today he's found literally from coast to coast, although not in the Southeast. Like the bobwhite, the pheasant thrives in edge habitat; he almost must have agriculture for food sources—but he also must have places to nest and escape cover.

In the Soil Bank (a federal soil conservation program) days of fifty years ago, the pheasant thrived; my father remembers seeing the skies black with pheasants over the grain fields of 1940s South Dakota. Today, with the relatively new Conservation Reserve Program (CRP) coming on line, the 1990s should see a tremendous resurgence of pheasant numbers.

Even so, there is outstanding pheasant hunting in many areas, and depending on the cover, there are many ways to hunt these beautiful birds. Great runners, they're tough for a big-running dog to handle. But close-working pointing breeds (and flushing dogs, for that matter) can work ring-necks exceedingly well in the creek bottom or shelter-belt cover these birds love.

The classic pheasant tactic, of course, is for larger groups of hunters to work grain fields. Here, a hunter or two will act as blockers at one end while the main party strings out in a line and works the field toward them. *Very* close-working dogs can assist in this effort, but out-of-control dogs will merely flush the birds out of range. The drivers should move back and forth, never moving in a straight line; the cool nerves of rooster pheasants are amazing, and they will allow a hunter to walk right past or will double back if they can.

Pheasants are neither hard to kill nor hard to knock down, but they must be properly hit in the head or front part of the body. Just tail feathers, and the bird will not be found. Retrieving dogs are a great assist, but careful shooting, concentrating on that white neck ring, is even more important. Experienced gunners often rely on number 7½ shot, concentrating on head shots. But most hunters feel number 5 or number 6 shot from modified-choke-guns are the best all-around choice.

The other two common imports, Hungarian partridge and chukar, are much more spotty in distribution. Chukars love rough, rocky, inhospitable country, while Huns prefer edge habitat around huge grainfields. Huns, known for wild flushing and rapid flight, are generally taken as bonus birds by pheasant hunters and western grouse hunters, although they can be hunted effectively in several northern states. Chukars have become a cult bird in the canyon country of Idaho and Oregon, but they are actually quite widespread, being found as far south as California's Mojave Desert and through much of Nevada.

Migrating Uplanders

The woodcock is a mysterious night-migrating bird, here today and gone tomorrow. He is generally hunted along with ruffed grouse, although a few students of the woodcock follow him for his own merits. The woodcock offers sporty shooting, usually taking off in an odd upward spiral—not so difficult as ruffed grouse, but still a plenty tough target.

The doves, including the common mourning and whitewing dove of the Mexican border, and the wild pigeons—the bandtail of the Pacific coast and the blue rock of Mexico—are migratory birds, pure and simple. But they're taken in the uplands with upland game guns. Shooting is generally pass shooting, whether adjacent to feeding or watering areas, and it's always sporty. The turning, twisting flight of doves makes them among the more challenging shotgunning targets. But wild pigeons, coming high on the wind, just may be the most difficult shotgunning target in North America. In both cases, the only dog work possible is retrieving for downed birds, and that's invaluable. For doves, number 8 shot is just fine, but the much tougher wild pigeons call for number 7½ or, at longer ranges, number 6.

Chukar hunting is like sheep hunting—hard work and lots of it. The secret is to locate birds, then get above them and hunt down. *Nobody* tries to hunt chukar from below; they'll simply outclimb you. The rocky terrain is hard on dogs' feet, but

The ringneck pheasant, originally from China, is so successful an import that many hunters forget they aren't native. First thought to have been released in the Wilamette Valley of Oregon, wild pheasant populations are found today in suitable habitat from the Atlantic to the Pacific, with greatest concentrations in the Corn Belt states of the Midwest.

© Kenneth Martin/Amstock

The mallard duck, above, called *greenhead* because of the drake's distinctive plumage, is North America's most prized duck, found in every flyway from coast to coast. Right, more and more modern waterfowl hunters are turning to the duckboats favored by our grandfathers for reaching secluded hunting spots.

close-working dogs are invaluable for chukars, especially for retrieving downed birds. The ideal chukar gun is *light*, with the three-inch magnum 20-gauge being a good choice.

Waterfowl

It's often said that there is more game in North America today than when the pilgrims landed, and in many cases, it's true. Whitetail deer are certainly far more plentiful, and possibly wild turkey as well. These species, plus all upland birds thrive in the edge habitat that man creates. But waterfowl, especially ducks, are in serious trouble. Lengthy drought in the northern nesting areas coupled with a century of wetland development along North America's coasts have seriously reduced our duck populations. Geese have fared better and, in fact, are doing better than ever. But today's trend toward shorter duck seasons and more strict bag limits is a sign of the times and isn't likely to get better. The population is huntable and indeed needs the hunter's attention and his dollars to turn this around. But these days, duck hunters need to savor their time afield more than ever before.

Waterfowl hunting generally takes one of three forms: hunting over decoys, pass shooting, and jump shooting in fields or small impoundments. Let's look at each.

© Will Brewster

© Will Brewster

Decoying, above, the most traditional of waterfowl hunting techniques, is a time-honored art. Coupled with the skillful use of a call, the goal is to bring the birds in very close, making the actual shooting almost an afterthought. Sea duck hunting, far right, on the cold northern Atlantic coast is a sport only for those willing to brave the elements.

Decoying

This is the most classic and traditional form of waterfowling, a game for the purists of the sport. It requires considerable skill on several levels. First, the proper site for a blind must be selected, overlooking a natural spot where passing flocks will wish to rest or feed. The blind must be built, then camouflaged perfectly. Pit blinds are good choices on level ground, while dugout blinds let into the bank may be the best choice along a river. A blind may take almost any form whatsoever, including simply lying in a field with a camouflage net pulled over—but it must hide you from sharp-eyed birds. And birds *do* see colors.

Next comes placement of decoys. The hunter must organize his spread so the blind is the least conspicuous from the ducks' point of view as they circle—yet their landing point must be well within range. Decoys and decoy spreads are an art form. Sometimes a few are enough, while in some areas, hunters use many dozens. How many depends on the country, the wariness of local birds, and the competition—whether flocks of real birds in a nearby sanctuary or the spreads of other hunters.

Finally comes skill with calling, essential to ensure that high-flying birds will notice the decoys. Calling waterfowl is also an art; not only of learning the right sounds, but learning when to call and when not to call. Today's hunters are fortunate in that there are a great many fine instructional tapes, records, and even videos that help them learn the right sounds and how to use them. But only experience makes a truly successful caller.

If the blind is well camouflaged, the decoys fool the birds, and the calling lures them in, then the decoying hunter is happy. The shooting is very much an anticlimax in this type of hunting—and indeed it's the easiest shooting to be found in waterfowling.

Steel shot will be required for almost all waterfowling today, but it is most certainly adequate for decoying birds. Most hunters place range stakes at whatever maximum distance they are comfortable with, never shooting beyond the marker. Forty yards is a good limit for decoying birds, and at that range, even with steel, the 20-gauge shooting number 3 or number 4 shot is adequate. Geese take a bit more shot; even over decoys they're a game for heavy 12-gauge loads with steel BBs. Waterfowling's behemoths, tundra swans, can be readily decoyed, but these birds require the heaviest loads and the largest shot that your gun will pattern.

A good retriever, trained to take a line and work to hand or whistle signals, is a good partner in a duck or goose blind. Not only will a well-trained retriever recover long-sailing hit birds, but watching a good dog work is also much of the enjoyment of this type of hunting.

Pass Shooting

For many hunters, the problem with decoying is that it requires a reasonably private location. Many public waterfowl areas do indeed offer good blinds, assigned by draw, thus ensuring separation from your neighbors. But equipment is also needed—often a boat, certainly decoys. And not all circumstances lend themselves to decoying. Sometimes birds will typically come off a refuge and head straight to a feeding area that is protected by law or is inaccessible to hunters. Deliberately ambushing birds along movement patterns is pass shooting. But under any circumstances, birds that will not decoy but fly within shotgun range may be taken by pass shooting.

This is not the purist's game, but it isn't the beginner's game, either. Its great pitfall is the temptation to shoot at birds that are too far away, thus risking wounding a bird and losing it. This is a game for experienced hunters who can judge distance, instantly determining whether a bird is at fifty-five yards and in range, or at sixty-five yards and out of range. It's some of the most difficult shotgunning in the world, a game for the heaviest loads in 10- and 12-gauge magnums, choked as tight as possible while still holding an even pattern. As an example of the difficulty of this shooting, the average lead required to hit a passing duck or goose at sixty yards is fourteen feet!

© Hanson Carroll/FPG International

The secret to pass shooting is to scout bird movement and try to position yourself where a great many birds are likely to pass. Use camouflage, natural or manmade, to stay out of sight, and forget the birds that are too high. Sooner or later, a flock will come by just a little bit lower, and you'll have your opportunity. A good retriever is extremely important in this type of shooting, for even perfectly hit birds may sail a long way. A good deal of goose hunting, and most sandhill crane hunting, is done by pass shooting.

Gear for Waterfowlers

Serious waterfowlers typically are gadget freaks—and the industry has responded with an incredible array of equipment designed specifically for them. Decoys come in a myriad of styles, sizes, and configurations, including some that even "swim"! Then there are decoy carriers, waders, parkas, hats, duck boats, and at least ten thousand kinds of calls. Clearly it would be easy to go broke just getting started waterfowling!

The beginning waterfowler must have a good set of chest waders, a tight-choked shotgun (preferably 12-gauge), a minimum decoy spread for the kind of waterfowl he wishes to hunt, and a good call. Next to the shotgun, decoys will be the most significant investment. Ask around to find out what *seems* to work best in your area. Sometimes inexpensive (and lightweight) silhouettes will work fine, but in other areas, full-bodied decoys are needed. For most duck hunting, a couple of dozen full-bodied mallard decoys are a good starting point. Pay attention to the details such as having anchors and anchor lines that allow the dekes to bob naturally and touching up the paint as required to keep your decoys lifelike. When setting up your decoys, remember that birds will land into the wind; you'll want to leave room in your set for birds to land well within range.

With a call, a little knowledge is a dangerous thing. The biggest mistake most duck hunters make is to overcall. Unless you are extremely experienced in calling, once the birds are working your way, shut up and let them come!

Jump Shooting

Ducks, and even geese, often sit in impoundments that are simply too small or too isolated for reliable decoying. And of course they may feed in grain-fields. Jump shooting in these locations, though not the technical sport that decoying is, can be productive and a great deal of fun.

It's a game for the stalking hunter, and indeed the best jump shooting is done just like spot-and-stalk big-game hunting. Feeding or resting flocks are often spotted from afar with binoculars, then a hidden approach is picked out. The idea is to stalk in as close as possible. Then, when in range, stand up, flush the birds, and be ready for fast action.

The shooting is a bit more difficult than it is when you decoy ducks, though ranges remain short. When a flock of ducks or geese get up, pandemonium reigns. The hunter must stay cool and pick his bird. And in the case of ducks, must quickly pick a bird of the right sex and species. In areas where there are many small farm ponds, jump shooting is a great deal of fun. Likewise, jump shooting along a winding river system—either on foot or by canoe—can provide exciting action. Murphy's law dictates that if there is water, birds will fall into it, so a retriever—kept at heel until the shooting starts—is nearly essential. Failing that, chest waders should be worn—and I must admit I've gone for more than one swim in freezing water to retrieve a jump-shot duck!

The wild turkey, possessed of amazing eyesight and hearing, was Ben Franklin's choice for our national bird. Although the wild turkey almost disappeared from much of his original range, his comeback ranks as one of conservation's greatest success stories. Today, the various subspecies of turkey are found coast to coast, from southern Canada to Mexico.

Wild Turkey

The wild turkey is the largest of all game birds and also one of modern conservation's most marvelous success stories. In just a generation, the wild turkey has been returned not only to almost his entire original range, but today he also occurs in huntable numbers in areas where historically there were no turkeys at all.

In the fall, turkeys are hunted much like a very large grouse—or by splitting a flock and then calling them back together. Ah, but the spring hunt. That's *turkey hunting*, when the gobblers are gobbling and searching for hens. Spring turkey hunting is the fastest growing of all the hunting sports, and for good reason. First off, it takes place in the spring, when few other hunting seasons interfere. Second, and most important, calling in a spring gobbler is one of the greatest thrills in the hunting world.

Although the wild turkey is indeed a bird, this is the one case when birds and bird dogs do not go together. The wild turkey is the big-game bird. Hunting him is a one-on-one game, requiring more hunting skill than many, perhaps most, four-footed big-game animals.

It is perhaps stretching a point to credit the turkey with high intelligence; he is, after all, a bird. But he is a wary bird, with unbelievable eyesight and keen hearing. If you make a mistake, whether in sound or movement, your turkey will be gone.

Turkeys can be spotted and stalked—rarely. And they can be ambushed—also rarely. The classic means for hunting a gobbler is to call him to the gun—a difficult, exciting, and demanding sport. It starts early in the morning, long before dawn, when the turkey hunter prowls the woods listening for a gobbler to gobble from his roost. Often, just when there's a hint of gray, the hoot of a barred owl will cause an old turkey to sound off.

Once a gobbler is located, the game begins. Clad in full camouflage, the hunter finds a comfortable, hidden location some distance from the roost tree. He makes the soft clucks and yelps of a hen turkey, using any one of a dozen different kinds of turkey calls. When the hunter is very lucky, the gobbler comes straight from the roost to him, and the game ends very quickly.

But it's more common that something else happens. A real hen gets in the way. Or, in the perverse way of old gobblers, the turkey goes the other way. Then it's time to relocate, either on that gobbler or another that's sounding off down the hollow a ways. The very sound of a turkey's gobble sends chills down the spine, and it's the rare hunter who can control his shaking hands when the bird struts into view, tail fanned out and head blood-red with lust.

Turkey Loads

Wild turkeys are very big, very strong birds. Poorly hit birds are only rarely recovered, but that's a tragedy easily avoided by taking only close and sure shots.

Most experts rely on head shots at an absolute maximum of 30 to 35 yards; 40 yards is a very long distance to shoot a turkey. Depending on how their gun patterns, most hunters rely on the heaviest possible load of number 6, number 5, or number 4 shot for that critical first shot.

Unfortunately, a fair number of turkeys are only stunned by the first shot. Two things are very important: to get to your downed turkey quickly and to be ready to back that first shot up *instantly* if the bird starts to get up. The second shot will almost certainly be a body shot, so most hunters use number 2 (typically the largest shot allowed by law) shot for the second shot. The biggest mistake turkey hunters make is hesitating to make that backup shot. Once a turkey starts to run away, you must shoot through the heavy back and tail feathers to reach the vitals, and your chances of preventing the bird's escape are very slim.

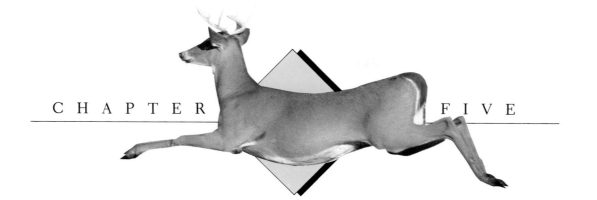

White-tailed Deer
North America's Favorite

Hunters will always hunt; as we have seen, it's a part of their being. But how they spend their time afield changes with the times. During North America's pioneering era, our wildlife resources were badly misused; the very concept of conservation as we know it today only came into being around the turn of the century—almost too late for many game species.

In the United States of the early twentieth century, all big-game populations were very low, and deer had almost—or completely—vanished from most states east of the Rockies. The American hunter from about 1900 into the 1930s was likely to be a duck hunter, for America's waterfowl populations were unbelievably high. Regrettably, there remained uncontrolled market hunting—and then

came the disastrous drought of the 1930s, the "Dust Bowl." Market hunting was finally halted, of course, but it was many years before waterfowl populations began to rebound from this dual assault—man's and nature's.

In the 1940s and 1950s, farming practices were slanted toward preventing another Dust Bowl. Fencerows and hedgerows were left thick and brushy, and the Soil Bank kept many fallow fields growing wild with perfect upland bird habitat. Hunters in this period were most likely to be searching out pheasant, quail, or grouse.

Starting in the 1960s, farming practices became ever cleaner, as the old hedgerows and brushy ditches were cleaned out to make way for agribusiness. More and more land in the South was shifted

The white-tailed deer is easily the most popular and probably the most populous game animal on the face of the earth. A creature of edge habitat, amazingly adaptable and able to live in close proximity with man, the whitetail is more numerous today than ever before, with a North American population believed to number around 20 million.

from row crops to tree farms, and throughout the United States, it became increasingly difficult for the bird hunter to knock on doors and be granted permission to hunt.

Conditions were no longer ideal for upland birds or their hunters, but the white-tailed deer population literally exploded. Throughout the eastern United States, the white-tailed deer experienced a resurgence as unprecedented as it was unexpected. More and more states began to list deer populations exceeding the 1 million mark—and seasons became longer every year to help keep the herds in bounds.

Suddenly hunters became deer hunters, a trend that continues to this day. And well it should, for the United States' whitetail population is climbing rapidly toward 20 million, with seasons in many states running to several months and liberal bag limits. I have seen this shift among my own hunting partners. Kansas had no modern deer season prior to 1965, and deer hunters were a most rare breed when I was growing up. But today all my old quail-hunting buddies have gone the way of the whitetail.

The West retained its historic deer and other big-game populations much better than the earlier-settled East, so deer hunting was always the traditional sport of western hunters. The native deer are different in the West: the mule deer of the breaks and mountains, their cousins the blacktail of the northwestern forests, and the diminutive desert

whitetail of the southwest. But the whitetail are moving west, too. Every decade sees them expanding their range farther and farther west, up river drainages and down valleys, so the whitetail is slowly becoming a western favorite as well.

Methods for hunting the traditional western deer are very much dictated by the terrain the various deer inhabit, so we'll discuss western deer in the next chapter. Here we'll concentrate on the white-tailed deer, the most numerous and most popular game animal in the entire world.

The adaptable white-tailed deer ranges from just below the tree line in Canada south to the Amazon basin in Brazil. Across this vast expanse of terrain, biologists have identified some thirty-eight different subspecies of whitetail. Obviously he varies greatly in size across this huge range: A 300-pound buck from Canada, Maine, or Wisconsin might be three times heavier than the average Florida, Carolina, or Texas buck. But they're all whitetails, and while the terrain varies, the animals' habits vary only a little.

Part of the secret of the whitetail's proliferation—and indeed its very survival—is its adaptability. Not only can it survive in virtually any habitat, but it also survives amazingly well in close proximity to man. It doesn't need much space; in areas with good food sources and plenty of water and cover, a white-tailed deer will usually live its six- to eight-year span and die within a square mile of where it was born.

White-tailed deer are habitual users of the same feeding and bedding grounds and the trails between them—this is one of their few weaknesses, and hunters exploit it. But their bedding grounds are likely to be in the thickest cover available, and their response to even a small amount of human pressure is to leave this cover only under cover of darkness.

All of the whitetail's senses are extremely acute; its hearing and sense of smell are second to none. And while its eyesight is not on a par with that of sheep and pronghorn antelope, the whitetail is especially attuned to pick up movement. That ultra-keen nose is the whitetail's first line of defense. If it hears or sees something suspicious, it just might hesitate until its nose confirms danger, but one whiff of human scent and it will unquestionably be off.

The vast majority of whitetail bucks harvested nationwide are unsophisticated youngsters, bucks from one and a half to three and a half years of age. Bucks who survive to full maturity learn from experience—and their defenses are nearly complete. Living in as close proximity to man as they do, the secretive white-tailed deer offer not only North America's most widespread hunting opportunity today but also its greatest challenge. And the specific search for a fully mature whitetail buck is a sport without parallel, exceptionally difficult and thus tremendously rewarding.

© Carl R. Sams, II/Dembinsky Photo Associates

Literally millions of North American hunters list deer hunting as their favorite pastime, and for most of them, "deer" means whitetails. This buck, left, a nice 10-pointer with typical conformation, is a long way from record dimensions, but is a fine trophy in almost any whitetail woods—and possesses marvelous eyes, excellent hearing, near-supernatural sense of smell, and innate cunning that makes all of his tribe a worthy challenge.

Traditional Hunting Techniques

Deer hunting is so popular today that much research has gone into whitetail behavior. Much of this information has benefited the hunter, both directly and indirectly, and has resulted in technology and techniques our predecessors never dreamed of. Even so, there remain three tried-and-true hunting techniques that still work: *still hunting, stand hunting,* and *driving.*

Still hunting and stand hunting are often confused. Still hunting doesn't mean sitting still, but rather moving through whitetail cover very slowly and carefully, trying to see deer before they see you. This is without question the most difficult whitetail hunting technique of all, for in that cover a human's senses are no match for a whitetail's.

There are ways to gain a very slight edge. First, follow the three-step rule. Take three steps, stop, look, and listen. *Really* look and listen, scanning the brush ahead with binoculars. Don't look for whole deer. Instead look for a shiny muzzle or eyes, the glint of an antler, the horizontal lines of belly or back against vertical trees and brush. Listen for the slightest sound. And be ready!

Still hunters simply must move with the wind in their face or, at the least, to one side or the other. But watch for deer that circle to get your scent! Besides hiding your scent, a slight breeze makes the woods slightly noisy and covers the noise of your

movement. Still hunting is most practical early in the morning and late in the afternoon, when deer are likely to be moving as well, and the noise of their own movement will make them less likely to hear yours. At such times, if possible, the hunter should keep the low sun to his rear, so a deer has to look into the sun and can't see as well. Still, regardless of the sun, the wind is the most important factor to consider.

Still hunting is difficult under all conditions, but with noisy ground cover, such as dead leaves, and in very thick cover, it is almost impossible to "get the drop" on a whitetail with this type of hunting. A recent rain or fresh snow ups the odds. Very slow movement helps, too—no more than a few hundred yards in an hour. It's fun to try, but the chances of succeeding at still hunting are slim.

Which is why stand hunting has evolved as the single most popular deer-hunting technique. Stand hunting is what it implies—finding a good place where you can stand still and stay put, waiting for your buck to come to you.

The most important element in stand hunting is picking the right place, thus *scouting* is the key. A stand may overlook feeding areas or active trails between feeding and bedding grounds. It can overlook a buck's scrape line or an active rub. Or it can offer a fairly broad vista in good deer country.

Depending on the terrain and vegetation, a stand can be in a tree, in a man-made tower, or

Stand hunting has become the method of choice for the vast majority of deer hunters. Elevated tree stands not only aid visibility but also help get human scent off the ground and away from the deer. The old adage was that deer don't look up, but don't count on it today. With so many hunters using tree stands, today's white-tailed deer do indeed look up—and often!

© Craig Boddington

There is much truth to the statement, "He who sits the longest gets the deer." A stand can be as simple as a comfortable tree to lean against, but the secret is to pick the location well, believe in it, and have the patience to wait and watch. In areas with hunting pressure, sitting still increases the odds of other hunters inadvertently moving deer your way.

other structure. It can be a ground blind. Or it can simply mean leaning back against a tree stump overlooking a trail.

Tree stands are extremely popular today for several reasons. In many cases, they offer the best visibility, and certainly they're safer in hard-hunted whitetail woods. If high enough, they also get a hunter's scent up off the ground and disperse it. But forget the old saw about deer not looking up! Today's deer have been hunted from tree stands so long that they do indeed look up, and frequently!

Whatever type of stand is used, it must be situated with regard for the prevailing wind, and the hunter must sit still and be vigilant. In general, he is counting on the deer's natural movement from place to place to bring a buck past him, but he can help that along with some of the modern techniques we'll discuss later. In areas that are hunted fairly hard, the axiom is that "he who sits longest gets the deer." Other hunters in the woods will indeed move deer, and the hunter who stays on his stand has a good chance to capitalize on this human-caused movement.

Natural movement will generally be during early morning and late evening only—but not always. During the rut, there is much more movement at all times of the day. And deer can "pattern" hunters in the same way hunters can "pattern" deer. If, as hunters are prone to do, the hunters in your camp are becoming bored with not seeing deer and are heading to camp in midmorning, consider staying on your stand through the midday hours. It could be that the deer realize that the woods are quiet between 10 A.M. and 2 P.M. and wait until that period to move around. Never be afraid to vary your pattern.

Sitting on a stand and allowing strangers to drive deer past you is a time-honored tradition, and so are more deliberate deer drives—they're almost an art form in many deer camps. The basics of a drive are simple: to place blockers or standers along one edge of a limited piece of cover and to have other hunters push through toward them, hoping to move deer.

There is no way to control how deer will move— or if they will move at all. A wise old buck may lie still and allow the drivers to pass right by—then slip out the back door. Or they may slip out between the drivers. But if everything works right, some deer will move past the blockers and present a shot. Whatever happens, it's an exciting way to hunt deer—and also a potentially dangerous one.

To conduct a drive safely there has to be one leader who stations all the blockers and sets the direction for the drivers. Every participant must know where everyone else should be, and every person must hold to the plan. In some cases, the drivers may be allowed to fire at deer that slip past them, and in other cases, they may not fire at all, but will change places with blockers on the next drive. But those who are cleared to fire must understand what direction is safe. Blaze orange clothing is a must, as are cool heads all around.

Given these safety precautions, deer drives are extremely successful. There are also endless variations, not only large affairs but also two- and three-person drives through limited or linear pieces of cover. If driving has a drawback, it's that this is generally a poor way to hunt really large bucks. A mature buck has seen it all and is most unlikely to go the way you want him to. And if someone does see a great buck on a drive, rarely will he present the opportunity to judge him properly or to get a good shot. In fact, although fine bucks are taken, through both luck and skill, by any method during any time of the hunting season, the best chance occurs during the mating season.

The Whitetail Rut

A big buck never loses his caution altogether, but he is most likely to make a mistake—or simply to show himself during daylight hours—when he has does on his mind.

The timing of the rut varies considerably throughout the whitetail range. In Alberta, it normally occurs in November; in Alabama, it's in January. At its very peak, when a preponderance of the does are in heat, the activity is frantic, with bucks literally chasing does throughout the woods. But

Fresh antler rubs, used by bucks to polish antlers and leave scent as territorial markers, are clear signs that a buck calls the area home. Massive rubs like these found in central Alberta are good news to any whitetail hunter—the buck that made them is well worth seeing.

Much remains to be learned about whitetail communication, but it's accepted today that deer are much more vocal than previously believed. Depending on the local pecking order, or dominance factor, a buck like this with his neck swollen from the rut is extremely likely to respond to a well-blown grunt call.

© Craig Boddington

long before the rut, there will be significant activity, and the whitetail hunter can read the sign like a road map.

Rubs, where the whitetail buck has polished his antlers (and left scent from the preorbital glands in his forehead), will start to become evident. Then the hunter will find scrapes—disturbed ground where the buck has urinated down over his hocks and pawed a clear spot on the forest floor. There is almost always an overhanging branch above the scrape where the buck has also left his scent. Both rubs and scrapes are only partially understood, but it is accepted that bucks use them to mark their territory—and that they will return to tend a scrape.

Prior to the rut there is the sparring match, generally between fairly well matched bucks. And when the rut is in full swing, there can be full-blown battles over who gets to mate with a particular doe, although serious fights are relatively

uncommon. Most of the modern deer-hunting techniques revolve around taking advantage of whitetail rutting activity.

High-Tech Deer Hunting

The first "magic" technique to draw a lot of national attention was horn rattling—the use of deer antlers clashed together to simulate fighting bucks. The technique originated in Texas, where hunters have known for years that a third buck might come to see what was happening if he heard two bucks fighting.

Today it's well documented that bucks will come to the rattling horns in all parts of the country. However, rattling is not necessarily a foolproof method (not that any such thing exists!). To work reliably, the local herd should have a relatively high buck-to-doe ratio, meaning that there will be competition among the bucks for does in heat. The rut doesn't have to be in full swing. In fact, rattling might work best before the hard rut, when just a few does are in heat and thus an amorous buck is more likely to pay a call. And of course the method plays upon a buck's curiosity as to why other deer are fighting in *his* territory. Unfortunately, the very largest bucks seem reluctant to come to the horns; very few record-class whitetails have been taken in this fashion.

Horn rattling is relatively simple; it's just a matter of clashing two antlers together in simulation of

a fight. Most rattlers also rake a nearby bush to simulate a buck's action in horning brush and also slap the ground with the back of an antler, as a buck would stamp his foot. As with most deer-hunting techniques, excellent instructional tapes and videos are available.

While rattling is a good adjunct to still hunting, other new techniques and gadgets are used by stand hunters. Chief among these is the incredible proliferation of scents and lures on the market today. Not all of these, of course, are for use during the rut, but many are.

Some are made from doe urine and are designed to attract a rutting buck to what he believes will be a doe in heat. Others use the opposite approach: to convince a dominant buck that a challenger has intruded into his domain. Many hunters use these buck scents to create a "mock scrape," issuing a clear challenge to a local buck. Then they put their tree stand overlooking this signpost and wait to see what happens.

Besides sex lures, there are two other general categories of scents—food attractants and scent masks. The former may be essence of acorn, apple, or whatever. Their intent is not necessarily to attract deer, but rather to mask human scent. If such a mask is chosen, it should be obvious that the scent must be natural to the area.

Scent masks may be as innocuous as pine, but are more likely to be something really horrible like fox urine or skunk scent. Do they work?

If a whitetail buck is directly downwind of you, I doubt if *anything* will prevent him from getting your scent. But there are degrees of wind and degrees of scent. How many molecules of human odor does it take for a whitetail to smell you? Nobody knows. The various scent masks do seem to help, but are *not* a guarantee of success. Most hunters today believe in them as just one of many useful tools.

Perhaps the newest rage to hit the deer-hunting market is the deer call. Whitetail vocalization is little understood, but it is now accepted that deer are extremely vocal. And today every call manufacturer offers a tremendous range of deer calls.

Most are extremely easy to use; the sounds a deer makes are soft and guttural and not difficult to reproduce. The danger, as with every other type of calling, is to overdo it. And also, as with every other type of calling, there are good instructional tapes available. I have had surprisingly good results imitating the fairly deep grunt of a mature buck with a grunt tube. Using this sound, I have seen deer I would not have seen—and I've shot bucks I would never have seen. Other hunters prefer a softer doe grunt or even a fawn bleat. But the deer calls are worth experimenting with. They don't work all the time, but they work.

Undoubtedly, the white-tailed deer will remain our top game animal for quite some time. Pursuing the whitetail is the favorite pastime of millions of Americans; to them, "big game" means white-tailed deer.

Tips to Prevent Spoilage

The biggest factor in game spoilage is body heat, and dissipating it as quickly as possible is your primary goal in caring for just-killed deer and other large game. There are several things to do to accomplish this. But first, here's one thing you shouldn't do: cut the animal's throat. There is absolutely no benefit to cutting an animal's throat after it's dead; much of the blood will have collected in the chest cavity after a typical body shot and will not drain through the jugular. However, cutting the throat *will* ruin a trophy for potential mounting!

I believe that the insides should be removed as quickly as possible, on the spot. Others prefer to bring an animal back to camp whole and perform those chores there. In cool weather, there's no problem with this approach, but I prefer to do it quickly anyway. Field dressing shouldn't take more than three to five minutes, and I've got friends who can beat sixty seconds every time.

I start by turning the animal on its back, then cutting away penis, testicles, and urinary tube down to the anus. (In some states, evidence of sex must be left on the carcass, so check local regulations. If that's the case, leave the sex organs on the carcass.) I then cut around the anus in a circle, freeing the end of the intestine.

Next step is to *carefully* make a long incision from the base of the sternum to the pelvis, making sure you don't perforate the stomach while you're doing this. I start with a very small incision, then place the index and middle fingers of my right hand (I'm left-handed) inside the opening, facing up. With the backs of those fingers I push the stomach and intestines down. Then, with the edge up, I place the blade of my knife, in my left hand, between those fingers and *gently* lengthen the incision until the body cavity is open from sternum to pelvis.

The diaphragm is located roughly at the base of the sternum. Working close to the rib cage, cut the diaphragm free in both directions. Now you will have to reach deep into the chest cavity (roll your sleeves up and put your watch in your pocket) to free the heart, lungs, and trachea. This is easier if you cut at least partway up the sternum. A knife will do it, but take care not to cut toward yourself—this is where people injure themselves badly. And don't go too far if you intend to mount your trophy; no more than three or four inches.

You will have to cut the trachea free, and this is the other dangerous operation. You'll

© Craig Boddington

be working blind with wet hands, so a small, controllable knife is best. I grasp the trachea with my right hand, pull it tight, then carefully ease my left hand with the knife past and cut the trachea as high as possible. Now it's a matter of dragging all the innards clear. You might have to cut the diaphragm a bit more on the backbone, and you might have to work your knife around the anus a bit more to free all the tissue. But if you've done everything properly, all the innards should come out complete, with no spilled stomach matter. Take care not to puncture the bladder; it will come out last. Drag everything clear, then save the heart and liver. I carry small Baggies for them.

I usually lay the carcass, opening down, over a bush to drain for a few minutes. I only worry about washing out the cavity if the stomach or intestinal contents spilled inside, but others feel the cavity should be washed out as quickly as possible. More important is to get the carcass cooled. With larger animals, propping the cavity open with a stick is important, and if possible, hang it so the air can circulate.

In warmer weather, the animal should be skinned quickly, again to aid in dissipating the heat. Make sure you have a game bag made of cheesecloth or cotton (old bed sheets made into a sack aren't bad!) to keep flies away. After skinning, make certain you take a saw and cut the sternum all the way down. Then open the neck the rest of the way down and remove all of the trachea. Failure to do this is one of the primary causes of spoilage.

Big Game, Big Country

The North American continent holds some of the most varied terrain on earth. From plains to forests to mountains, from searing desert to frozen tundra, the diversity of our wildlife habitat is staggering. And in these wild lands roam a stunning array of magnificent game animals, each offering its own unique challenge to the hunter.

Aside from white-tailed deer, there are the mule deer and black-tailed deer, and their larger cousin, the stately elk. And that's just the beginning. The wild lands of North America are shared by a quartet of bears and another of wild sheep; by moose and caribou, pronghorn and musk-ox, mountain goat and cougar, bison and more. Let's look beyond the whitetail's woodlot to North America's game country, seen through the eye of the hunter.

To the hunter accustomed to pursuing whitetails in eastern woodlots, the vast wilderness regions of the American West and Canada are as unfamiliar as the moon—and appear just as rugged. Planning and preparation are required to hunt true wilderness, but that's where much of the continent's most interesting game is found.

The Great Plains

When Lewis and Clark journeyed westward, they discovered a vast sea of grass, and on those grassy plains roamed a wealth of wildlife unequaled by even the Serengeti Plain in Africa: bison, the American buffalo, by the millions; pronghorn antelope, deer, and elk beyond counting; grizzly bear; and even what we now call mountain sheep in the river breaks. But the open plains proved fragile, and the game succumbed too readily to man's excesses. The sheep, elk, and grizzlies—those that were left—retreated to the high mountains, while the rest dwindled until few remained.

In this century, the situation has improved for many animals. Bison were saved from extinction, and pronghorn antelope were returned to much of their original range. With them returned the deer and even a few isolated herds of elk. Today a few scarce permits for elk may be drawn for in such unlikely places as Oklahoma, Kansas, and Nebraska; by special permit, too, there are opportunities to hunt bison. But for most of us, Great Plains hunting means pronghorn antelope and prairie deer—both whitetails and mule deer.

The pronghorn antelope is a uniquely North American creature, with no close relatives anywhere in the world. More closely related to the goat family than the antelope of Africa, it is one of the fastest animals in the world—and one of the most sharp-eyed. A beautiful creature, the pronghorn has

© Rod Planck/Dembinsky Photo Associates

It's believed that 60 million bison roamed the Great Plains in 1860. Turn-of-the-century hunter-conservationists, Teddy Roosevelt chief among them, saved the species, but the great herds will never return. Still, bison occur in huntable numbers in a few areas, opposite, for those who want to relive a bit of history. Mule deer, above, are surprisingly common in the plains and badlands east of the Rockies.

a buff-colored body with white underparts and a black nose to match its pronged black horns. It relies on its eyesight and speed to keep out of trouble. Hunting the pronghorn on foot, on its own wide-open ground, is a matchless experience—yet one that is well within the reach of today's sportsman.

Permits must be drawn for in a lottery to hunt pronghorn antelope, but they aren't difficult to get. Both Wyoming and Montana, where the bulk of the pronghorn population is found, normally have permits left over after the drawings are concluded.

Pronghorn hunting is a game of spotting and stalking. First a herd must be located, seen initially as tiny white specks through the mirage of distance. Good binoculars confirm that these are indeed pronghorn, and then the spotting scope comes out. The hunter may look over many herds before a stalk is attempted, but finally, at twenty-five power, a buck with long, hooked horns is seen. Then the real fun begins. An unseen approach must be found, which seems impossible at first

glance. But there are hidden folds in the seemingly flat prairie. It might take belly-crawling through cactus, but you'll find a way to get within range. Or perhaps you'll wait by a waterhole; bowhunters often use pit blinds with life-size pronghorn decoys.

Both whitetails and mule deer share the pronghorn's prairies, sometimes occurring in the same area. The mule deer roam the rolling sagebrush hills and are hunted in much the same way as the pronghorn—with binoculars and on foot. Whitetails, on the other hand, are creatures of the timbered watercourses and must be hunted in the same way whitetail are hunted everywhere. But local hunters tend to ignore them in favor of the more easily hunted mulies, and prairie whitetails are some of the largest of their kind.

Going after pronghorn antelope on the plains of eastern Wyoming was my first big-game hunt, and it remains one of my favorite outdoor adventures. The clean air and vast open spaces are in themselves worth the journey, but the pronghorn dotting those plains make it a most special experience.

The premier plains game today is the pronghorn antelope, liberally dotting the plains of the West. Fleet footed and sharp eyed, stalking this attractive animal in the open country he calls home is a matchless experience. Typically, a nice buck is spotted from afar using good optics, and then during the stalk, *tiny* folds and ridges in the seemingly flat country must be used, which often requires crawling on hands and knees between sharp-spined prairie cactus.

© Craig Boddington

The Western Mountains

Early fur trappers called the Rockies the "Shining Mountains," and even today they're the Promised Land for American hunters. High and rugged, America's western mountains offer limited permit hunting for prizes such as bighorn sheep, Rocky Mountain goat, and Shiras or Yellowstone moose. Here, too, houndsmen pursue mountain lions, and black bear roam the high valleys in good numbers. But the animals that draw most hunters to the high country are elk and mule deer.

The foothills and plateaus are fine game country and often can be reached by four-wheel drive, and then productive hunting can be done on foot. But the true wilderness—and there's still a lot of it—can only be reached the hard way, on foot with backpacks or on horseback. This is the essence of Rocky Mountain hunting, which is rarely easy, but offers some of the world's most magnificent country as its own reward.

Whether you chose to hunt afoot or on sturdy mountain horses, on your own or with an outfitter, mule deer are hunted almost exclusively by spotting and stalking. These western deer are more nomadic than whitetails. In autumn, they may range the same general area until snows push them to winter pasture, but they cannot be relied upon to use the same trails and bedding areas. Finding a

© Will Brewster

A truly large Alaskan moose, like this record-class bull, left, is an awesome creature—the largest deer in the world, carrying the largest antlers of any animal in the world. But when a creature like this is brought down, the real work starts—packing on foot. It took three long days to bring out all that marvelous moose meat.

Use of saddlehorses, above, is a traditional and enjoyable way to hunt the western mountains, greatly increasing the amount of country you can see and hunt. Horses, too, are a tremendous aid in packing out downed game—a real consideration when hunting game as large as elk. The secretive cougar, right—usually seen only with the aid of trailing hounds—is surprisingly common in western North America.

© Sharon Cummings/Dembinsky Photo Associates

© Skip Moody/Dembinsky Photo Associates

Excellent game management has brought bighorn sheep, above, back to huntable numbers throughout much of the West. Permits are generally extremely limited and highly sought after, but a great ram is a possible prize today for those who persist. Far right, six points per side is the typical configuration of a fully mature bull elk. Many believe that a large elk is one of the most difficult prizes in modern hunting.

good buck is usually a matter of painstaking glassing, using a good vantage point to cover the big country with clear binoculars.

Early-morning and late-evening bucks may be spotted on the move, feeding, and, late in the season, chasing does. At midday, favorite places to glass are under rimrock, where bucks feel safe in knowing they can see any approaching predator. And indeed, in their high-country haunts, bucks seen at long range may or may not be approachable by a man on foot.

In years gone by, mule deer were considered much easier to hunt than whitetails, but this is no longer true. More sensitive to man's encroachment than whitetails, mule deer—especially mature, trophy-class bucks—will never again be as plentiful or as easy to hunt as they were just a quarter century ago. And today's bucks are hunter-wise, every bit as savvy as a big whitetail. Accurate, flat-shooting rifles are essential, but the real keys to hunting mule deer today are time, patience, and stout legs. The big bucks are there, but they don't come easy today, and there are no shortcuts.

Elk (properly though not commonly known by the Algonquian name, *wapiti*) are a huge deer, easily twice the size of even the largest mule deer or whitetail. With senses as keen as any deer's and with long legs that will carry them to the next mountain range when spooked, elk are among the world's most difficult animals to hunt. And a mature bull, one with six points per side, is one of nature's most majestic creatures.

A century ago virtually the last remnants of a once-huge population had retreated to the newly created Yellowstone Park. In the early years of this century, that Yellowstone herd provided a nucleus for reintroductions throughout the historic elk range. Today the elk is again numerous, with stable or building herds in all of our western states and western Canada as well. But the big bulls, never easy to come by, form an increasingly smaller percentage of most herds today.

Elk are hunted by a variety of methods, depending on the season. Perhaps the most classic of all elk hunting occurs during the rut, when the lilting three-note challenge of one bull to another echoes through the canyons. This "bugle" can be readily imitated, and under the best of circumstances, a rutting bull will literally charge the call, prepared to do battle. Often, though, he will answer but move away, especially if he is already with cows. Sometimes a stalk or an ambush is then possible, but however it works, a tremendous advantage is achieved in getting a bull to answer the challenge.

The great beasts are indeed vulnerable enough during the rut that fewer and fewer opportunities

Prime time to hunt elk is early in the fall, when the bugle of rutting bulls splits the clear air. Late season, after the snow flies, elk are herded together and there's usually a tracking snow. In between, after the rut and before the onset of winter, hunting is usually at its most difficult—but the autumn colors in the mountains are their own reward.

exist to hunt them at this time. A few bugling rifle seasons remain, but most states restrict hunting during the rut—usually in September—to archers. And indeed, with today's know-how and superb archery equipment, the bowhunter who takes advantage of these seasons has excellent odds for success.

Elk hunting, which never is easy, becomes much more difficult after the rut has ended. No longer is there a chance for a bull to come to the hunter nor will his eerie call reveal his presence. Instead, it's a game of glassing in the high alpine basins or painstaking still hunting on timbered ridges. This is the time when most fall seasons are held, and the hunting is rarely easy.

On the other hand, the mountain air is crisp and clear, and the aspens and western tamarack have turned golden. It's a beautiful time to be in the mountains, and the elk are there for those who

hunt hard enough and have luck. There are some new tricks that work, too. As with whitetails, elk vocalization has been widely studied in recent years. And indeed elk, especially the cows, are extremely vocal, and not just during the rut. They communicate reassurance and alarm via soft mewing. This "cow talk" has become extremely important to close-cover elk hunters. Easy-to-use calls and good instructional materials are readily available, and this is a technology that should be in every elk hunter's repertoire.

Later on, after the snow flies, there is a third type of elk hunting in the many areas with long seasons. The snows may or may not push the elk down to lower, more accessible elevations, but wherever the elk go, they must leave tracks. It's tough hunting then because it's very cold and the going in thigh-deep snow is torturous. But the timber is quiet, and visibility is better through the bare branches. Elk are beginning to concentrate, too, toward winter pastures. It's good elk hunting, some would say the very best, but only for those in good shape.

However you choose to hunt the western mountains, one of the things you must always keep in mind is how you will pack out your game. Unlike in so much whitetail country, even on the open plains, chances are you will not bring your four-wheel-drive close to your kill. And don't even try to drag a downed bull elk anywhere! Horses are a good answer to the problem. If you don't have them, a pack-frame is the other option. Some hunters carry two elk quarters, but the average hunter in tough country only carries one at a time. That makes four to six trips for an elk, two for a hefty mule deer. The distance you can carry your game out is the limit that you may hunt, pure and simple. Foolish is the hunter who pursues elk or high-country mulies without a firm plan for bringing back the game.

© Rod Planck/Dembinsky Photo Associates

The northern forests are difficult to hunt, especially for hunters accustomed to more open country. The ability to read signs is extremely important.

The Northern Forests

The forests of the northern United States and southern Canada are part of a forest belt that circumnavigates the globe in the Northern Hemisphere. And indeed much of the game in this region has close cousins in the Old World. Our moose, for instance, are subspecies of the moose of Finland. And for that matter, even our elk is biologically the same species as the red deer of Europe.

Moose are found throughout the forested region of Canada, dipping down into the United States in huntable numbers in Maine, Minnesota, and the Rocky Mountain states. Elk, while primarily high-country animals today, are well distributed in the forests of the Pacific Northwest, and there's even a small relocated herd in Michigan.

In general, mature forests are not the best deer habitat, because they offer little browse in the understory. But white-tailed deer range throughout the northern forests, from the Atlantic west to eastern Washington and British Columbia. In the Rocky Mountain states, they share this sparse habitat with a few mule deer, while in the more lush forests of the Pacific Northwest, the black-tailed deer, a small mule deer subspecies, thrive.

Almost as adaptable as white-tailed deer, the black bear is also found in the swamps of the Deep South and in virtually all of North America's mountain ranges. But he's most typically a creature of the northern forests, shy and largely nocturnal, and an omnivorous feeder able to subsist on anything remotely edible.

The forests are difficult to hunt; visibility is limited, walking often noisy, and without snow, the forest floor is a poor tracking medium. Glassing is practical only where there are openings, whether natural clearings or clear cuts, and where the topographic relief offers visibility. Still hunting is perhaps the most universal hunting method for antlered game in the timber, but it is also easily the most difficult method. The utmost in woodsmanship is required to get close to game animals without spooking them, and even when this is accomplished, getting a clear shot is rare.

Stand hunting is without question the most practical method for whitetails, with preseason scouting to determine movement patterns extremely important. If the rut coincides with hunting season, calling is effective for both elk and moose, the latter called in by imitating the call of a lovesick cow moose. And, perhaps because of the thicker cover they live in, black-tailed deer are much more receptive to both calling and antler rattling than their mule deer cousins.

In general, the antlered game found in the timber may be hunted by the same methods used to hunt their tribe in other habitats, but the lack of visibility makes everything much more difficult.

© Craig Boddington

Hunting the great bears of the north, above, is the dream of many hunters. The grizzly and Alaskan brown bear are among the few truly dangerous North American animals— especially in close cover. Although found from the high mountains to the open tundra, moose, right, are typically creatures of the forest—a true giant among deer, with the largest bulls weighing up to three-quarters of a ton.

© Michael Havelin

The mule deer, right, is the deer of the West, found in various subspecies from the Great Plains to the desert and from the high mountains to the forests of the Northwest. The type of mule deer found in the far Northwest is the small blacktail, shown here in the rugged Olympic Peninsula. Far right, a monarch of an Ontario moose. The moose, the largest deer in the world, is another species found in Europe as well as North America.

© Stan Osolinski/Dembinsky Photo Associates

This is the major problem with hunting the black bear, which perhaps is more at home in heavy timber than any other animal.

Black bear hunting is a uniquely regional sport, with hunting methods that are preferred in one area being not only avoided, but often illegal in another. Depending upon which part of the country you're in, the favored technique might be spotting and stalking, running with hounds, or baiting. In mountainous country with broad, open hillsides, glassing for bears—spotting and then stalking—is popular and productive. But in the forests, either running with hounds or baiting are the only practical options beyond hoping for a chance encounter —and the odds of simply running into an animal as shy and wary as a black bear are beyond remote.

Hound hunting, for both black bear and mountain lion, is a popular pastime in many areas where these animals are found, but it is frowned on as an unsporting activity in many others. To the houndsman, the excitement of following the music of his pack is everything, and indeed actually shooting a bayed bear or cougar is quite simple. The dogs do the work. To the hunter the challenge is twofold:

first, training and controlling the hounds and lead-
ing them to a fresh track; and, second, keeping up
with the pack wherever the chase leads. This can be
difficult in any terrain, but is especially so in heavy
cover.

Baiting for bears is especially practical in heavy
cover and, in areas where it's practiced, has almost
developed into an art. Placement of the bait is critical, because the shy, nearly nocturnal bear must
have the confidence to step from cover to feed
while shooting light remains. And placement of the
stand or blind is even more critical; it must be
close enough to offer a sure shot and camouflaged
so as to allow the hunter's slight movement—and
placed so the bear can approach without winding
human scent.

While following a bear trailed by hounds can be
physically demanding in the extreme, waiting for a
baited bear is a game of nerves and patience. Typically, the hunter will go to his stand in the late
afternoon, because bears are far more likely to feed
in the evening than the morning. Then the long
wait begins, with hours sometimes stretching into
days. And finally, when the light is fading and every
black shadow turns into a bear, the real one
appears. Perhaps you hear a twig snap, but more
often than not there's no sound and no warning—
the bear simply is *there*. And you must try to control your racing heart while you try to determine if
he's the kind of bear you're looking for.

© John Gerlach/Dembinsky Photo Associates

© Tony Mandile

Desert plants are fascinating and beautiful—but most are thorny propositions. Desert deer and javelina, amazingly, eat a wide variety of cacti—but humans are much thinner-skinned. We have to watch our step in the desert, and always carry tweezers to pull out thorns.

The Desert

There are deserts and then there are deserts. Some, like the interiors of the Mojave and the Sahara, are too dry to support large mammals. But most of our southwestern deserts are living deserts that support a surprising variety of wildlife well adapted to survival in such arid lands. Amid the stately saguaro cactus, mesquite, murderous cholla, and a hundred other thorny plants, the coyotes, jackrabbits, and sidewinder rattlesnakes share the desert floor with javelina and desert mule deer. In the rocky hills above are desert bighorns and Coues whitetail—and the mountain lions that feed on them. A surprising number of black bears, too, thrive amid the scrub oaks and desert grass.

The desert bighorn, with its small body and big horns, is without question one of this continent's greatest game animals. Sadly, hunting it is an experience few will enjoy today, for only a handful of the sought-after permits are issued annually. The desert deer, javelina, and even the cougar, however, are readily huntable today, and their pursuit offers a rare opportunity to experience the desert's beauty as well as its harshness.

The mountain lion, of course, is hunted almost exclusively with well-trained packs of hounds—though a few hunters have brought them in with predator calls. Only in the Southwest, too, is a predator call an accepted means among hunters for bringing in black bears—and indeed some of the

© Tony Mandile

largest black bears ever recorded have been taken in this region by that method.

Glassing for bears is also extremely productive, especially in the early fall, when bears are feeding on the ripe fruit of the prickly pear cactus. And glassing is virtually the only technique used for hunting desert deer, both mulies and whitetail, and the little javelina. This is big country, where canyons stretch away endlessly, game is thinly distrib-

uted, and powerful binoculars and skill in using them save endless miles of fruitless walking.

In the deserts of northern Mexico, glassing is productive, to be sure. But down there, local hunters have learned to track mule deer on the desert floor. On this dry, often rocky ground, this is a skill that must be seen to be believed—but it yields some of the largest-antlered mule deer being taken today.

The deserts of the Southwest, seemingly barren and forbidding, hold incredible numbers of wildlife. However, large mammals are widely distributed in this big country, so the hunter must be prepared to cover vast distances. Nowhere else are good optics so critical.

© Carl R. Sams, II/Dembinsky Photo Associates

The North Country

As we have seen, great hunting for an amazing diversity of birds and big game can be found from Mexico to the Great Lakes, from the Florida swamps to the Pacific Northwest—and everywhere in between. Whether swamp, forest, desert, or high mountain, all hunting country is beautiful in its own way. But to the north, the wilds of Canada and Alaska beckon to the hunter, and there awaits not only some of the greatest true wilderness remaining on earth, but also some of the world's most magnificent animals.

From the island of Newfoundland to the vast expanse of Alaska roam the largest of the deer tribe, moose, and also, above the tree line on the endless tundras, vast herds of the nomadic caribou. On the tundras of Canada's Northwest Territories and her Arctic islands, caribou are joined by the unique musk-ox, and on the pack ice above, polar bears roam. Farther west the ubiquitous black bear gives ground to his larger cousin, the grizzly, and along Alaska's southern coasts and islands roam the Alaskan brown bear, king of the grizzly tribe. The mountains of northern British Columbia are home to the salt-and-pepper Stone sheep, while the northern mountains are dotted with the pure white of Dall sheep. Mountain goats, too, roam the windswept crags in sometimes incredible numbers.

The northern wilderness of both Canada and Alaska hold a variety of game deserving of the hunter's fascination. Caribou, above, are perhaps the most accessible of the northern game. Although Alaskan brown bears, right, are thinly scattered and offer more limited hunting, they still represent the ultimate dream for many sportsmen.

© Craig Boddington

This moose camp in Alaska,
above, was Spartan but
comfortable.

A traditional horseback hunt in Canada's Yukon is one of North America's greatest adventures. With two weeks or more of hunting for Dall sheep, moose, caribou, and grizzly bear, such hunts have changed very little in this century. Similar trips can be found in Alaska, northern British Columbia, and the Mackenzies of the Northwest Territories—and nowhere else in the world.

These animals and more haunt the dreams of any hunter—but there's also the lure of adventure. Any hunt to the north country is indeed an adventure, a journey into the harsh realities and stark grandeur of untouched wilderness. The hunting skills that must be applied change little, whether they involve glassing for caribou on the open tundras or sheep on treacherous shale slides—or still hunting a mighty bear along a salmon stream. But the excitement of hunting unfamiliar animals in untrammeled country is unmatched, and the beauty of such country cannot be equaled.

Hunting the north country is hard work, whether it's a lung-burning climb to glass one more sheep basin or a thigh-aching slog across a muskeg valley to get a closer look at a bull moose. It's serious work, too, for the mountains can be steep, slick, and dangerous—and the weather is always treacherous, waiting to pounce on the unready. Unlike hunting in the lower forty-eight, the game can be dangerous, too; the great bears of the north must properly be rated among the most dangerous animals in the world, and rutting bull moose have been known to charge freight trains.

North-country hunting can vary from a week's hunt for caribou or moose to a full-blown expedition for sheep, grizzly, or a variety of species. Virtually all northern hunts are guided, a legal requirement that has few exceptions. Perhaps this is just as well, for the logistics as well as the potential pitfalls indeed merit the services of a professional guide/outfitter.

Thus, to some extent, a hunter's budget must determine his planning of a hunt. But other considerations must be taken into account. In some areas, primarily in western Canada, horseback hunts are prevalent. In others, particularly on the tundras, where the ground is far too spongy for horses' hooves, all travel will be on foot. The hunter must honestly evaluate whether he is up to the miles and miles of hard walking that might be required—and either get in shape or find other options. Beyond horses, there is some potential for hunting by floating down rivers or traveling by boat along the shores of large lakes. And in coastal Alaska and British Columbia, some of the best bear and even goat hunting is done by glassing the bays and inlets from large motor launches, then going ashore and making a stalk when something is spotted.

Important, too, is having the best clothing and gear available—for nowhere is the weather less forgiving than in the Far North. And yet it's fat country, too; the lakes and streams offer some of the finest fishing, and there are usually ptarmigan and waterfowl to add to camp fare. It's marvelous country with marvelous game, offering a lifetime of memories. As with so much hunting far from home, much of the memories are of a fine camp and outdoor experiences shared and lessons learned from a competent guide.

Horseback Hunting Tips

Seeing the mountains of the Canadian or American West by horseback is one of the most enjoyable ways to see the country, and having horses available to pack out game gives hunters far more options than they have on foot. However, hunters who are inexperienced horsemen can have their dream quickly turn into a nightmare.

Riding—especially the long, rough-country rides required by wilderness hunting—uses different muscles than walking, running, or other forms of exercise. The better overall shape you're in, the better off you'll be. But if you're embarking on a horseback hunt, get out to a local stable and spend a little time in the saddle beforehand. Every bit of riding you can do will help.

Getting saddle sore is a real potential problem. Old hands used to wear panty hose, but today lightweight polypropylene long underwear—or silk—will work just as well.

Don't be afraid to tell your outfitter that you have no experience with horses—or that you're afraid of them, if that's the case. Many people are afraid, and the outfitter will be able to plan his assignment of horses accordingly. Most mountain horses—though certainly not all—are gentle and accustomed to being ridden by unfamiliar hands.

Hunters who do a lot of horseback hunting acquire their own saddlebags, rifle scabbards that fit their rifle, and oversize stirrups for use with hunting (vice riding) boots. Most outfitters have basic gear they can get by on, but few invest in such niceties. Inquire about these items, and put a saddle scabbard on your Christmas list. There's nothing worse than a long ride with your slung rifle banging across your shoulders!

Follow your outfitter's directions regarding your horse, but in general obey these rules.

- Never let go of your horse if you get off. Tie him up, hand him to someone, or hang on to him!
- Never walk away from your horse having left your rifle in the scabbard. Take it with you, or if you must leave it somewhere, hang it in a tree well away from your horse.
- In general, give your horse his head and let him pick his own way in rough country. *But* if he starts to stumble, keep his head up.
- If you feel like you're going to lose it or your horse is going down, concentrate on two things: Get your feet clear of the stirrups, and bail out on the uphill side.
- If you get nervous or scared, *get off* the horse.

SEVEN

Hunting Camps, Hunting Guides

To most hunters, camp is a very special place, a deep-rooted part of the hunting tradition. In many parts of the world, the hunting camp is a very permanent arrangement, carefully maintained, added to and improved over the years, and passed on from one generation to the next. Camps such as these—be they log cabins, tar paper shacks, or simply a location where the tents are put up come hunting season—are often and perhaps most traditionally deer camps. But the camp's residents could just as easily be duck, elk, goose, moose, quail, or turkey hunters. The type of game isn't so important; what's important is that the owners of such a camp have a common interest and a permanent place to hunt that draws them hither year after year.

It is in such camps that parents teach their children lessons about hunting and about life. And hunters fortunate to grow up visiting such camps will carry to their graves fond memories of the camaraderie found there. Such camps exist wherever in the world there are hunters. I've enjoyed the hospitality of a Pennsylvania deer camp—quite possibly the archetypal permanent hunting camp—but I've seen the same clapboard shack, the same good humor, and sampled the same camp fare with New Zealand duck hunters and with kudu hunters in South Africa. Thus it is that many young hunters the world over undergo their rites of passage as hunters in the company of established groups of their elders—and in the setting of a traditional camp.

Hunting camps may be plain or fancy, but they're always home. The poles for this simple tent camp, left, on the shores of a Northwest Territories lake were flown in with the tent, because nothing that stout grows so far north. It wasn't much, but proved dry and warm and added to the memories of a great hunt.

A retreat such as this is, of course, just one of the innumerable forms that a hunting camp may take. To a backpacking hunter, camp is wherever you lay your head, and for traveling hunters, camps range from comfortable lodges to pup tents on a windswept glacier. But whatever form the camp takes, it's an essential part of the hunting experience.

It's from the camp that you sally forth every morning, and it's to the camp you return. You praise or damn the cook, take your turn at washing dishes, brag about your great shot—or take the requisite ribbing if you miss. And you partake of perhaps the oldest hunting tradition of all, that of sitting by the fire—whether a wood stove, a fireplace, or an outdoor hearth of circled stones—far into the night, swapping tales of other hunts in other places, arguing over the perfect gun and load, and laying plans for the next day's hunt.

Hunters who enjoy their sport close to home or who hunt on their own without hiring outfitters or guides generally create their own camps, tailoring them to their needs and desires. For some, this may mean a permanent arrangement, like we discussed above. For others, a motel room may offer a perfectly acceptable camp, for still others, a lightweight backpacker's tent and sleeping bag. Depending on the situation, sportsmen who spend a lot of time afield probably use a wide variety of camps.

But when you're planning a long-range trip and must use the services of an outfitter because of distance, logistics, or the simple legal requirement to be guided, you have the option of selecting the kind of camp you want to hunt from. Some hunters don't care; so long as there's enough to eat and a dry place to sleep, that's just fine. Other hunters *do* care, and it's fine that they do; the camp is truly an important part of any hunt. You see, no hunting trip is certain. No outfitter can control the weather; it can be horrible and assure that the only thing you see *is* the camp. Nor can an outfitter guarantee how the game will move. And for darn sure he can't guarantee how well the clients will climb the mountains or how straight they will shoot.

In fact, the only thing an outfitter can really guarantee is a good camp. Your idea of a good camp may not be the same as mine, but when you're shopping for an outfitter, you really owe it to yourself to consider the kind of camp you're happiest in—and make certain what you're arranging will suit your needs.

The options are endless. For example, you want to try an elk hunt in the western United States. Let's say you're an experienced outdoorsman, and you want a classic elk-hunting experience—and you're in good physical condition. You should consider a horseback hunt into a true wilderness area. That means a tent camp, probably a whitewall affair in one of the designated wilderness areas in the Rockies. A matchless wilderness experience, yes, but not inexpensive, and not easy either, because in wilderness areas game movements are weather sensitive. You will hunt hard and have the time of your life, but taking an elk is hardly a sure thing. To some extent, hunting success is dictated by how hard you can hunt and how well you can shoot under pressure, but it would be rare that your odds for success exceeded 60 percent.

Now, let's be honest. You have a desk job. You aren't in the best shape, and you haven't ridden a horse in twenty years. You've hunted whitetails all your life, and you want to hunt elk. You also want to bring an elk home from that hunt. If this is the case, perhaps you should consider an elk hunt on private land, where you'll hunt from a comfortable lodge, sometimes on horseback, but most of the time in a four-wheel-drive. You won't enjoy the quality wilderness experience of a traditional elk hunt, or its miseries, but you'll have a great hunt, and your chances for success are probably increased to 80 percent or higher.

Or let's say that you want to make a hunt in Canada or Alaska. You aren't sure exactly what you want, you just know that you want your next hunt to be in the north country. As you investigate outfitted hunts, you'll quickly understand the laws of supply and demand. Sheep and bear permits are scarce and in high demand, so those hunts are very expensive. If that's what you want, go for it, but if

© Craig Boddington

© Will Brewster

The wall tent, left, is the traditional camp in the western mountains. If it has a good stove and is tied down securely, a good tent will serve through the worst weather Mother Nature has to offer. Some outfitters, however, offer permanent lodges—often with the lodge as a base only, with the hunting done from remote spike camps. These moose and caribou hunters, above, have returned from spike camps with their game and can relax in the lodge's relative luxury.

you just want to experience the north country, consider moose or caribou.

Then start considering your physical condition and desires, and the conditions of the hunt. If you still want a sheep hunt, early on you must choose between a backpack hunt and a horseback hunt. Backpack hunts aren't for everybody, and it's foolish to undertake one unless you *know* you can walk and climb all day carrying a pack that weighs at least fifty pounds. Remember, guides aren't packhorses. They hike and hunt all the time, and thus can carry more than you, but no guide can carry all his gear, plus yours, plus your ram when you get one. Horseback sheep hunts are easier, if you're willing to spend long hours in the saddle in rough country. And of course, with either option, you'll spend your nights in a rough tent camp (often just a sleeping bag laid out under a tarp). To some that's *fun*, but to others, it seems better to enjoy the beautiful country with somewhat less physical hardship.

If you want to see the country, but breaking your tail in the process doesn't sound sensible, then sheep hunting and most certainly goat hunting are poor choices. Other poor choices might include some types of bear hunting and even moose hunting on foot, where the carcass may need to be packed some distance. But there's good bear, moose, caribou, and even occasionally goat hunting from boats or within reasonable proximity of com-

fortable lodges or cabins. Even a few of the top horse outfits have established permanent cabin camps in their areas.

A common pitfall is to believe that abundance means ease of hunting. Elk, for instance, are, after deer, the second most abundant large-game species on the continent—but hunting them is far more difficult than hunting many less numerous game animals.

African hunting will be covered in more detail in the final chapter, but it should be said here that choices regarding camps, outfits, and animals to be hunted must be made for foreign hunting trips as well. In Africa, the decision to seek a traditional tented safari, a ranch hunt, or a hunt from a permanent lodge is one of the basic considerations; it will dictate the price range of your safari and often even what countries you can consider. Nor is all the hunting in that vast land equally easy. Forest hunting, for instance, is extremely arduous, requiring miles of walking in tropical heat. Likewise elephant hunting. On the other hand, many safaris remain practical for older hunters.

The bottom line is that most hunting can be as difficult or as easy as you wish it to be. If you're in shape for the toughest hunts, you have a *slight* chance of taking a bigger animal. But if you're not in shape for the tough ones, your odds for success will be much worse than if you undertake only hunts you're physically capable of handling.

Horses are invaluable aids for hunting much of North America, especially the western mountains. For those who live elsewhere, the availability of riding stock and packhorses is a very real reason for hiring a guide. Other reasons, equally good, include knowledge of the country, availability of places to hunt, and the full range of logistical considerations.

When you're planning a long-distance hunt, to a large degree you're putting your dreams, dollars, and chances for success in the hands of a guide. In some cases, you can control who this individual is; perhaps someone you know hunted with him, perhaps you met him at a sports show, or perhaps you just know of him by reputation. All too often, though, you book your hunt with an outfitter and your hunt is in the hands of a guide who works for that outfitter and has been assigned to you.

Hunting guides run the full gamut, from serious professionals to the most rank beginners; from great conversationalists to sociopaths. Most are somewhere in between these extremes. Typically, they love the outdoors, and they're willing to accept ridiculously low pay to spend more time doing what they love. They may be surprisingly adept at making "dude" hunters comfortable and ensuring that they enjoy themselves (which is indeed part of their job)—or they may be totally lacking in any social graces.

I am personally what you might call a "professional client" as opposed to a "professional guide." I live in one of the world's largest cities, with no hunting country whatsoever in my backyard. I do some bird hunting and deer hunting close to home, and I make it a point to go on a few unguided hunts annually—first, because it's fun to do things your own way, and second, because I feel it's important to keep my hand in and my skills sharp.

© Will Brewster

The light airplane revolutionized hunting in Canada and Alaska. Once on the ground, the hunting is as it always was—but in an hour or so, a Super Cub with tundra tires, pontoons, or even skis can whisk hunters to country that would take many days to reach on foot or horseback.

But the vast majority of my own hunting is guided, not because it has to be, but because I don't have the time required to outfit my hunting in other states.

I have no count of the total hunts I've been on, but at this writing, I can list twenty-three different African hunts, fifteen in Canada, six in Alaska, three in Mexico, and that's just the beginning. All of these long-range hunts, plus others in Europe, the South Pacific, and the United States have been guided. I have personally never had a serious problem with a hunting guide.

That doesn't mean all my guides have been perfect. Many have been more knowledgeable than I, others less so. In recent years, sometimes much less so. Some have had difficult personalities. Some haven't spoken a word of English. But hunting guides are just people, and most streets run both ways. Hunting guides want their hunters to be successful and to have a good time, but they're a proud bunch. They don't want to be treated like hired help, and they simply must be allowed to feel that *they,* not you, are in control of the situation.

The hunting guide's primary job, and what you

should ask him to provide, is knowledge of the country and the local game. If you help with the camp chores—cooking, fetching firewood and water, washing dishes, tending the horses—you'll enjoy your hunt more, you'll allow your guide more time to *think* and *plan* the hunt, and you'll create the feeling of partnership that should exist between any hunter and his guide. But it's simply amazing to me how many hunters wander into a camp and expect everything to be done for them. Yes, they've paid for some level of service, but the most important thing any hunter can do to increase his chances of success is to help create that partnership between himself and his guide. Promises of a big tip may help, and indeed whatever tip you can afford is appreciated by the hunting guide; he works for low wages, and tips are important to him. But you can't buy a free-spirited individual like a hunting guide, and only a fool will try. Work *with* your guide. Help with the chores, and if you've got a better idea on how the hunt should be conducted, try to suggest it so that it's his idea— but only if you're damned sure you're right. After all, all things being equal, it's *his* country, and he

© Craig Boddington

should know what works. If you're certain he doesn't, try to find a diplomatic way to make a better suggestion.

However, after many years of watching hunters and guides and hunting camps, the biggest mistake I've seen hunters make is to waltz into camp insisting they know more than their guides. It's human nature, but downright foolish. If the outfit is good enough to hire, allow them to do their job. Only after you become *certain* you've got a better idea should you step in, and then only with tact and diplomacy.

Hunting guides run the gamut of society. Some are misfits, some are college graduates (and some of the misfits are college graduates, while some of the good ones are illiterate). The good ones are good with people *and* with game. The best way to ensure that you will share your hunt with a competent guide is to do your pre-hunt research with extreme care.

It's just like shopping for a car or any other major purchase. You see the advertising, and that's a lead, but you don't necessarily believe all the claims. You read magazine stories about an outfit, but you should keep in mind that even the most glowing account is just one person's impression. So you start your research.

The *Where to Go* advertising sections of any outdoor magazine offer a good starting point. You write to as many outfitters as you can find who seem to offer the area, game, and hunting conditions you're looking for. You ask specific questions about camps, hunting techniques, weather, and long-term success percentages. And then you *demand* references. *Call* those references, don't write them. Remember that only the most honest outfitters will offer hunters who were not successful as references. If you find a hunter who was not successful but still gives a good reference, chances are you've got a good guide.

But the most valuable information any reference can give you isn't whether the hunter was successful or not. *Ask* who else was in camp. Were they successful? How was the equipment? Can they recommend a specific guide you should ask for? What suggestions can they offer?

Most outfits, from Africa to Alaska and back again, are good. And most guides are serious, dedicated, enthusiastic, and fairly competent. The real secret to success on any hunt, however, is to do everything you can to have those qualities in equal measure. If *you* are serious about your hunting, dedicated to spending your time and energy at it, if you keep your enthusiasm in spite of adversity, and if you add whatever competence and hunting skill you have to offer—whether specific to the area, or simply shooting skill when the time comes—you will be successful. And if you're not, your guided hunt will still be a memorable outdoor adventure. And after all, that's what we're really after.

Safari
The Hunter's Dream

In the soft Swahili tongue of East Africa the word *safari* simply means "a going-forth," a journey. Indeed every hunt is a going-forth, even if only into the woodlot behind your house to collect a squirrel or rabbit for supper. But safari has come to mean so much more to the hunter: the very word smacks of excitement and adventure—the sights, sounds, and smells of the African bush. What hunter hasn't dreamed of seeing Africa's myriad antelope roaming the short-grass plains? Of stalking greater kudu in the thornbush thickets? Of his own moment of truth with a Cape buffalo or lion?

The dream can be dreamed by every hunter— and in these days of rapid transportation and instant communications, the dream is easier to realize than ever before. Africa has its problems, to

be sure. A burgeoning human population has pushed the game out in many areas, and poaching remains severe for animals with commercial value, especially the rhino and elephant. Yet in spite of these critical problems, sport hunting continues, and indeed must continue; more and more it is being realized and accepted that the dollar value placed on game by sport hunters is critical to their survival. The sport hunter brings in foreign currency desperately needed by African governments —and much of that money is used to finance anti-poaching efforts and habitat improvement. Even more than in our own world, in developing countries game must pay its own way if it is to be allowed to flourish. Carefully managed hunting programs are a partial answer, and of course sport

Africa is a land of surprises, with hunting country varying from desert to grassy savanna to mountains and forests. One of the most beautiful regions is the Okavango Delta of northern Botswana, a true wonder of the world created by the Okavango River diving into thousands of clear, flowing channels. The Delta is one of many great African hunting regions.

hunters are removing only a harvestable surplus. Today more than a dozen African nations include hunting programs as part of their game-management efforts.

Then there are concerns over personal safety while traveling in Africa. The last thirty years have seen an end to Africa's colonial era, and few nations have emerged without political turmoil and bloodshed. But most of the areas open to hunting are stable, and foreigners are more than welcome. Under the worst circumstances, hunters in Africa are usually safer than in many North American cities. The United States State Department and the Canadian Department of Foreign Affairs will advise travelers regarding areas considered unsafe, and the African governments themselves rarely allow visitors into areas where problems are likely. Sensible hunters will heed these warnings, and if they do, then the likelihood of any problem is exceedingly remote.

Finally, many hunters believe that African hunting is an unaffordable dream. As is the case with hunting for North American sheep and the great bears, the laws of supply and demand hold. Permits are extremely limited today for lion and elephant, as they should be. Thus the lengthy safaris required for animals such as these are indeed expensive. Expensive, too, are safaris into some of Africa's more remote regions; for instance, into the forests of central Africa to hunt bongo, a large forest antelope. Such hunts are logistical nightmares for the outfitters, and they are indeed astronomically expensive.

There is, on the other hand, a whole world of African hunting that remains surprisingly affordable. In fact, with jet transportation and good road networks over much of Africa, it's possible to enjoy a very fine safari for about the same cost as a moose hunt in Alaska.

Such a hunt would almost certainly be on a private ranch in the southern African countries of Namibia, South Africa, or Zimbabwe. The hunting would be for plains species such as kudu, impala, warthog, zebra, wildebeest, and more. Africa holds more than 100 species of plains game, each beautiful and interesting in its own way. The game availa-

The Cape buffalo, below, remains a possible prize in much of Africa's back country. Cover-loving, cunning, and downright dangerous, the buffalo offers some of safaris' greatest thrills.

© Craig Boddington

ble varies widely from one area to another, with some species, such as kudu and zebra, having a very broad range. Others, such as sable antelope and swamp-dwelling lechwe, are found in just a few areas. Some, such as South Africa's little Vaal rhebok and Ethiopia's mountain nyala, are found in just one very restricted area.

Every region has its common game and its local prizes as well. Most areas will offer a selection of somewhere between ten and twenty *different species* of game that may be hunted on a single safari—a wealth of game unknown anywhere else in the world. The wise hunter will study his African game well before his hunt, determining the animals that

are most important to him and learning what may be found in the area he wishes to hunt.

Typically these ranch hunts in southern Africa are conducted on private land of large acreage, not dissimilar to hunting pronghorn and mule deer on a ranch in Montana or Wyoming. The outfitter or rancher may establish a safari camp or lodge, or the hunter may stay in the ranch house. Such hunting is generally not physically demanding and will be very pleasant. The hunters will sally forth every day in a Toyota Land Cruiser or Land Rover, sometimes seeking something in particular, other times just seeing what the day might bring. The hunting may be done by glassing, tracking, or simply still hunting likely cover. Most hunting in southern Africa is conducted during the African winter months, June through September, when the nights and early mornings are crisp and the days sunny and warm.

The traditional African camp is a tented affair, comfortable and well equipped. Game is usually an important part of camp fare, and virtually all varieties of African game are delicious.

© Craig Boddington

Not infrequently, ranch hunting for plains game may be combined with leopard hunting, especially in Zimbabwe, where the spotted cats are amazingly common. But beware: Leopard hunting is a time-consuming business of baiting, checking baits, and spending long evenings sitting in a blind. The first-time hunter is often better off not concentrating his hunting time in an all-out effort to get Old Spots.

The only problem with ranch hunting is that it is not a traditional African safari. Circumstances where buffalo can be hunted on private land are rare and even more rare for lion. The hunter who wishes to enjoy a bit of old Africa—a tented camp where he can sit by the fire and listen to hyenas laugh and lions roar by night, and where he can track buffalo herds by day—needs to look elsewhere.

Traditional safari hunting, in vast game areas in Africa's hinterlands, still exists. The hunter in search of such an adventure will find it, but can expect to pay more. Without enormous expense he can plan a safari of seven to fourteen days that will include buffalo as well as a goodly selection of plains game. Such hunting might be in the more remote government concessions in Zimbabwe or it might be in Botswana, Zambia, or Tanzania. Such a hunt is perhaps the ideal compromise between a very inexpensive plains game ranch hunt and a full-blown safari that will include the cats. And hunting Africa's Cape buffalo is one of the most exciting and enjoyable adventures that continent holds.

While herds of buffalo are occasionally spotted out in the open in the early morning, the buffalo typically will feed out in clearings only at night, spending their days resting in the heavy thornbush. Most buffalo hunts begin with a search for tracks made during the night. Then the hunt is on, a tracking job that is often long and always exciting. When the buffalo are found, they will be black animals in black shadow, and the big bull must be sorted out from his herd of cows—or from the lesser bachelor bulls he roams with.

Buffalo are wary almost to the degree that white-tail, elk, and kudu are wary—but unlike deer and antelope, the buffalo can turn the tables. An unwounded buffalo will rarely charge, but the buffalo is not an animal that you can afford to make a mistake with. So you work in close, making sure you get the perfect shot. And all too often the herd smells, hears, or sees you, and they're off in a cloud of dust and thunder of hooves. Then the tracking starts all over again, but this time the buffalo are more alert than ever.

Hunting them as they should be hunted, on foot in the heavy thorn, is one of hunting's grandest experiences. And buffalo remain extremely plentiful in Africa's hinterlands. If you can't afford a buffalo hunt, by all means go on a plains-game safari and your dreams of Africa will come true. But if the budget can possibly be stretched to cover a hunt that will include buffalo, do it; there is no

The leopard, below, is shy and secretive and amazingly common throughout much of Africa. Of Africa's dangerous game, the leopard is perhaps the most available species—but hunting him is a most difficult, time-consuming, and thoroughly interesting business. This tent camp, far left, nestled under acacia trees on the Masai Plateau of Tanzania was a small slice of heaven.

The variety of African game must be seen to be believed. The species of antelope, for example, number into nearly the hundreds, with some very widespread and others restricted to just a few areas. The common impala, far right, is found throughout much of the continent. The sturdy gemsbok or giant oryx, right, are a desert antelope found only in southernmost Africa.

greater thrill, whether for first-time African hunters or old safari hands.

Hunts planned specifically for leopard will usually last ten to fourteen days. While leopards are always tricky and difficult to hunt, the hunter who spends that kind of time really concentrating on leopard in good country will probably be successful, but he or she must not be sidetracked by other game until the leopard has been taken. Good leopard hunting is extremely available today and can be done for little more than the cost of a plains-game hunt.

Lions are another story. Permits are scarce today, with most outfitters in lion country having just a small handful of annual licenses on quota. Lion hunting, too, is a specialized pursuit and can be quite time consuming. And since the permits are scarce, most outfitters exact a premium price for lion hunting or insist on a minimum number of hunting days, and sometimes both. A hunt of two weeks is quite minimal for lion, but if the hunter really concentrates on getting a lion, the chances for success are not bad.

Cat hunting, however, is best left to a full-blown safari of three weeks. With that amount of time, hunters can properly work on both lion and leopard, perhaps hunt more than one area, and have time to hunt buffalo and the local plains game.

Remote areas in Zimbabwe are excellent for such lengthy safaris, but as good or better are the classic safaris offered in Botswana, Tanzania, Zambia, and the northern savanna region of the Central African Republic. Such safaris are not for everyone, because they are indeed expensive; daily rates for such hunts, on a one-hunter-per-guide basis, average around $1,000 per day—four times the price of very fine plains-game hunting. And there will be air charters, licenses, and miscellaneous expenses as well. But the experience of such a safari and the memories it will offer are more than worth the money if you can afford such a hunt.

Under all circumstances, African hunting (and most guided hunting everywhere) is much less expensive if two hunters share a guide. The wisdom of that course is a question worth exploring.

In general, hunting partners sharing a guide should first of all be good friends who have hunted together enough in the past to understand—and overlook—each other's idiosyncracies. And long before the hunt they should agree on personal priorities and a *firm* system for who takes first shot when. Some hunters trade off by the day; others establish different priorities ("You get the first crack at a kudu, but I get the first shot at a sable").

If these details are agreed on, there's absolutely no reason why two hunters shouldn't share a guide on a typical plains-game safari. Under most circumstances, it's possible to take an average of one antelope species per day. Average meaning that, in most areas, plentiful herd animals such as wilde-

Today's African professional hunters—together with their trackers and skinners—continue a long and honored tradition of safari hunting begun, to a great extent, by Theodore Roosevelt on his historic 1909 East African expedition. Professional hunter Russ Broom and his crew, right, pose with a fine sable antelope. Below, it can be argued endlessly as to what animal is most dangerous. The author's vote goes to the lion—not only deadly but also one of the most magnificent game animals in the world.

© Craig Boddington

© Craig Boddington

beest, impala, hartebeest, and so forth could be taken almost at will—while opportunities for more elusive animals such as kudu, bushbuck, and eland might crop up only once every few days. It should all work out that each of two hunters, sharing a guide, could expect five to seven nice trophies on a ten-day hunt.

Buffalo safaris of ten to fourteen days, too, are good opportunities for two buddies to hunt together. It might take three or four days to get a shot at a good buffalo, but there will still be time left over for some plains-game hunting.

Cat hunting is different. This is a most specialized pursuit best done one on one, and any other way means that someone is likely to be disappointed. It is unusual to expect more than one opportunity at a lion or leopard in a fourteen-day hunt. The exceptions would be lengthy hunts in very good country or a situation where one hunter wanted a lion and the other wanted a leopard. This works out well, for most leopard hunting is done in the evening while most baited lions are stalked at first light—but it will mean very long days for the entire hunting party!

Africa is changing rapidly; the human population continues to expand at an alarming rate, and poaching is a very real problem. Black rhino hunting is a thing of the past, and the species' very survival hangs in the balance today. Elephant populations are stable or increasing in several countries, and elephant hunting remains open in a few places. Looking at the continent as a whole, though, the elephant is in trouble. Lions don't get along well with livestock, and available land for the great cats is decreasing annually. Buffalo, too, have been eradicated from vast areas due to the threat of hoof-and-mouth disease. For the foreseeable future, African hunting remains a possible dream, and without question the plains-game hunting will remain marvelous for many years to come. It's the old Africa that's shrinking—and if the dream of Africa haunts you as it does so many hunters, make it happen as soon as you can! But be careful. The dream of Africa can become an obsession, and most hunters will feel compelled to return.

© Craig Boddington

In open country, most African hunting is done by traveling slowly in a vehicle until game is spotted, then commencing a stalk. In thornbush and forest, tracking is the most common technique. In the swamps, however, transportation is usually the dugout canoe, poled through reedbeds and lagoons—a fine way to see a unique part of the world.

© Hanson Carroll/FPG International

The hunter's world hardly ends with Africa. There is still fine hunting on every continent. The forests and mountains of Europe, where the hunting is rich with centuries of tradition, are more accessible to outsiders than ever before. The outback of Australia offers great hunting for water buffalo, while the green hills and snowy mountains of New Zealand hold a variety of fascinating species imported from around the globe a century ago. South America offers some of the finest waterfowling on earth, along with her unique big-game species. Asia beckons to the mountain hunter, with races of wild goat and wild sheep that still haven't even been properly identified. And a whole world of hunting is opening up behind what used to be the Iron Curtain. Only the future will tell us what might be found in the wilds of Siberia and in Russia's vast mountain ranges. Perhaps future generations will dream of hunting the steppes of Russia as we have dreamed of Africa—but hunters will always dream of magnificent game in faraway places. And sooner or later, if they dream enough, adventurous hunters will find a way to make their dreams come true.

The hunter's world is wide, with varying customs and traditions. Although the dress may differ, traveling hunters find kindred souls the world over.

Hunting and Conservation Associations

The following is a partial listing of the national and international organizations fighting to preserve the sport of hunting and conserve wildlife resources. There are groups here that cater to virtually every type of hunting—and these are the kinds of organizations with which hunters everywhere need to become involved. Please note that memberships in those organizations marked with asterisks are by invitation only.

BOONE AND CROCKETT CLUB

241 South Fraley Boulevard

Dumfries, VA 22026

(703) 221-1888

CAMPFIRE CLUB OF AMERICA

230 Camp Fire Road

Chappaqua, NY 10514

(914) 941-0199

DALLAS SAFARI CLUB

Twin Towers, Suite M-17

8585 Stemmons

Dallas, TX 75247-3803

(214) 630-1453

DUCKS UNLIMITED, INC.

One Waterfowl Way

Memphis, TN 38120

(708) 438-4300

FOUNDATION FOR NORTH AMERICAN WILD SHEEP

720 Allen Avenue

Cody, WY 82414

(307) 527-6261

GAME CONSERVATION INTERNATIONAL

900 NE Loop 410, Suite D-211

San Antonio, TX 78209

(512) 824-7509

GRAND NATIONAL QUAIL HUNT CLUB*

P. O. Box 5039

Enid, OK 73202

(405) 233-5682

GRAND NATIONAL WATERFOWL HUNT CLUB*

P. O. Box 106

Cambridge, MD 21613

(301) 261-8300

HOUSTON SAFARI CLUB

4710 Bellaire, Suite 110

Bellaire, TX 77401

MZURI SAFARI CLUB*

5803 Dawn View Court

Castro Valley, CA 94552

(415) 886-5544

NATIONAL RIFLE ASSOCIATION OF AMERICA

1600 Rhode Island Avenue NW

Washington, DC 20036

(202) 828-6000

ONE-BOX PHEASANT HUNT CLUB*

851 South Second Street

Broken Bow, NE 68822

(308) 872-5941

ONE-SHOT ANTELOPE HUNT CLUB*

1880 Hillcrest Drive

Lander, WY 82520

(307) 332-9849

PHEASANTS FOREVER

P. O. Box 75473

St. Paul, MN 55175

(612) 481-7142

QUAIL UNLIMITED, INC.

P. O. Box 10041

Augusta, GA 30903-2641

(803) 637-5731

ROCKY MOUNTAIN MULE DEER FEDERATION

P. O. Box 748

Springville, UT 84663

(801) 489-8129

ROCKY MOUNTAIN ELK FOUNDATION

P. O. Box 8249

Missoula, MT 59806-8249

(406) 721-0010

RUFFED GROUSE SOCIETY

1400 Lee Drive

Coraopolis, PA 15108

(412) 262-4044

SAFARI CLUB INTERNATIONAL

4800 West Gates Pass Road

Tucson, AZ 85745

(602) 620-1220

SHIKAR-SAFARI INTERNATIONAL*

100 Country Club Drive

San Luis Obispo, CA 93401

(805) 528-8114

UNITED CONSERVATION ALLIANCE

1104 14th Street NW

Washington, DC 20005

(202) 789-0526

WATERFOWL USA

The Waterfowl Building

Box 50

Edgefield, SC 29824

(803) 637-5767

WHITETAILS UNLIMITED, INC.

P. O. Box 422

Sturgeon Bay, WI 54235

(414) 743-6777

WILDLIFE CONSERVATION FUND OF AMERICA

801 Kingsmill Parkway

Columbus, OH 43229-1137

(614) 888-4868

WILDLIFE LEGISLATIVE FUND OF AMERICA

801 Kingsmill Parkway

Columbus, OH 43229-1137

(614) 888-4868

WILDLIFE MANAGEMENT INSTITUTE

1101 14th Street NW, Suite 725

Washington, DC 20005

(202) 371-1808

WILD TURKEY FEDERATION

Wild Turkey Center

770 Augusta Road

Edgefield, SC 29824-1510

INDEX